The Ultimate Guide to Content Marketing & Digital PR

How to get free attention for your business, turbocharge your ranking and establish yourself as an authority in your market

BY:

Charlie Marchant

Luke Nicholson

Tim Cameron-Kitchen

EDITED BY:

Mitchell Labiak

Receive Lifetime Updates to this Book and Claim a FREE Review of your Website and Digital Marketing @ www.exposureninja.com/pr-book

ISBN 978-1534672956

Table of Contents

Why Teaching Myself Marketing Was The Best Business Move I Have Ever Made

Back in 2010, I was published in a magazine for the first time. I'd written a book about drumming (I was a professional drummer at the time), and sent it off to my favourite magazines hoping to get my name out there a little bit. The magazine had written a review of my book – which was nice and impressed my friends.

I didn't want to stop there though, I thought there was scope for more.

If the magazine's editors weren't going to write a longer article about my book, then I decided I'd do it myself. I wrote a long, interview style article, took a picture of myself by setting a camera on a timer, and sent it to a magazine asking if they wanted to publish it. It was a bit of a long shot. To my absolute amazement, they printed it as a double page spread, almost word for word. This happened four times in different drumming magazines around the world. I sold an unprecedented number of books, DVDs, and drumming courses as a result.

I immediately realised what the biggest companies have known all along: that strong marketing is the difference between commercial success and outright failure. But my experience proved that you didn't need to be a big company to be successful.

Fast forward two years and I was selling websites to tradesmen. I noticed that these tradesmen weren't really online much, but they *did* read lots of magazines. These magazines talked about everything except **how to get more**

customers. So I decided to crack open Microsoft Word again and write some articles about why tradesmen needed websites.

I found out the names of the editors and emailed my articles to them. About 50% of the articles I sent out were picked up and published. At the end of the article, I'd mentioned that readers could contact me if they were interested in getting a website. My phone went crazy for the next two weeks every time one of those articles was published.

The magazine world has changed immeasurably since 2010, and I'm not going to insult your intelligence by banging on about the 'digital revolution' or any of those phrases people use to explain what's blindingly obvious to anyone who hasn't been living in a cave with no signal. The good news with all of this is that the number of publications (I use the term loosely to include includes blogs, news sites, journals and online magazines) has increased exponentially.

Everywhere you look online there are places where your target audience is hanging out, hungry for more content. Whether it's tech geeks studying Wired and TechRadar or fans of long-gone railways reading inscrutable hobby websites, the internet has enabled viral publication growth by lowering the barrier to entry and allowing almost anyone to become a publisher.

What this means for savvy businesses of all shapes and sizes – from the one man bands like me back in the day to larger companies with huge ad budgets and ambitious growth goals – is that getting yourself in front of your target audience, wherever they are spending their time, is simpler than ever.

Journalists and editors who make decisions about what to write used to be difficult to track down. It was all 'meeting for coffee' and 'networking, networking, networking'. If you didn't have the connections, you couldn't get to the people that you needed unless you were willing to wine and dine.

Introverts rejoice! Now these journalists are on Twitter, right now, using hashtags like #prrequest and #journorequest to find people to feature in their articles. I've been featured in Forbes, the Telegraph and the Guardian *in the last 2 months* just through responding to a few Tweets. Enquiry services send out hundreds of emails a day from journalists looking for businesses like yours to talk to about pretty much anything – it's how we've got our clients on national newspaper sites and live on BBC TV. And you can do it all without even having to get dressed.

The visibility and credibility benefits of this new digital PR landscape are obvious: it truly is easier than ever to be seen in the sort of cache publications that instantly elevate your status in your market.

But visibility and credibility are not the only benefits of using the strategies in this book. In fact, they're not even the *primary* benefit for a lot of our clients. See, we originally started our digital PR department to get our clients' websites ranking higher. Google rewards businesses that are seen everywhere with better ranking, so getting yourself featured on lots of different websites grows your ranking, traffic and *business*. Later on, you'll read some case studies of businesses we have grown, launched and transformed using the exact same digital PR strategies that we'll be showing you. There are no secrets and we've held nothing back.

This book is a plain English, no experience necessary, step-by-step guide to making the most of the huge opportunity to grow your business using content marketing and digital PR. It's written mainly by Charlie and Luke, the super ninja double team that head up our 24-strong Digital PR department at Exposure Ninja. They're in the trenches doing this stuff day in, day out, working for our clients and developing new ways to make them known. I hope you find what they share valuable and I hope that you try it out yourself.

Remember that if you need any help with anything you read about in this book, we're here to help you. Visit our website at www.exposureninja.com and we'll be glad to give you a hand.

– Tim

Introduction

What is Digital PR and How can It Benefit My Business?

You've got a small business and you want potential customers to know about it. You've set up a website that looks pretty okay and registered your social media accounts, sharing a little bit of content here and there. There's maybe a dribble of traffic coming to your website, but in the big, competitive world of the internet, the reality is that nobody knows who you are.

How do you get your business noticed in a sea of other businesses? How do you hook in customers? You've got to get people talking about you. You've got to find what your target customers are reading and get your business some coverage on that website. You can work around the clock telling as many people that will listen about your business, and you'll still be just a drop in the ocean. But if the people that you're talking to start to tell their friends and then they tell their friends... you can be at the million mark in under fifteen minutes.

In this chapter:

- Why Small Businesses especially need a Digital PR Strategy
- How to use this Book to Run Your Own Totally Ninja Digital PR Campaign
- Why We Wrote This Book

In 2015, we started work with a performance management software company who provide software for HR teams in SMEs. They had a simple but effective website already up and wanted to build up their brand name before the official launch of their software which was still being developed at the time. The guy running the business was ahead of the game: he'd done his research, he knew the trends and his software was set to blow his competitors out of the water. But his business was new, it was small and no one had heard of them – yet.

We started building up a list of websites, magazines and blogs that were well read by HR professionals and reached out to editors offering articles about new trends in the performance management industry. We successfully placed content with a number of small but still influential websites in the sector. Smaller sites tend to be more receptive to receiving content from businesses and companies, especially ones which aren't well established. The value of smaller, niche publications should never be underestimated. These are the important foundations for a digital PR campaign.

Once our client's name and business had been featured on a number of different websites, we set our sights higher. We began pitching to the big boys in the HR industry, looking for publications where our articles would really start to get some traction. We sent editors links to our other published articles to show that this business really knew their stuff and would provide incredibly valuable content to these bigger websites.

Our content got accepted, we published more and more articles, and soon we struck lucky! One of our articles on new performance management trends in 2016 went up on Minutehack.com, an advice website for small business owners in the UK. The article got shared on over 400 social media shares, mostly on LinkedIn. The snowball had started. HR professionals began to pick up the article through LinkedIn and enquiries about the software and requests for demos began rolling in.

That same month, we spoke to a journalist from The Guardian's small business sector. They'd seen our client featured in a number of publications talking about effective management strategies and asked him to provide a quote for a feature being written on business success. Together with the client we wrote up a killer comment about managing performance and motivating employees. The comment was published in an article on The Guardian's website, including a link to the client's website.

Months ago, no one had heard of this company or the guy running it, and now he was in the UK's most authoritative online newspaper! Small acorns really do grow mighty oak trees.

Why Understanding PR Has Never Been So Important

PR is the art of creating and maintaining a favourable impression of your company among consumers and influencers.

It's become cliche to say that we live in a connected world. The average Briton spent two hours and fifty-one minutes online *every single day* in 2015, roughly equivalent to one in every six waking minutes. The younger generation, representing the media consumption habits of the future, spend more time online and less time in front of the TV than their elder counterparts. They have been dubbed the "cord cutters" for ditching cable in favour of the online streaming options offered by the likes of YouTube and Netflix.

Never before has it been so easy to have your message seen by so many people. Everyday more people are connecting to the internet and spending longer online, while innovative content creation tools are making it possible for anyone with something to sell to put together valuable and share-worthy content. Millennials get their political news not from newspapers or TV, but from Facebook – which by the way has 1.49 billion monthly active users. And it's not just millennials and teens, 63% of all Twitter's 300 million monthly users read the latest Tweets to catch up on the news too. Half of people under thirty-five view social media sites as being just as important sources of news as television and print.

But even more important than the amount of people using the internet, and treating it as a valuable source of information, are the connections and social groups that form online.

What's *most* exciting is not the big numbers, as very few businesses will have something that a billion people want. What's much more exciting is that these big numbers are built from millions upon millions of different niches. Whether it's Chihuahua owners, Chihuahua puppy breeders, or people who dress up as Chihuahuas at the weekend, if your audience shares a common interest, trait or goal, you can be in front of them within seconds. Wherever they live, whatever they spend their time doing, and whichever magazines they read – they're all there reading blogs and using social media.

At Exposure Ninja, we spend all day working with a range of businesses on the frontline. It's very rare – almost unheard of – that we'll see a market with more than a couple of players using digital PR, content marketing, and social media *really* effectively. Whether it's a lack of resources or an unwillingness to take the risk, your competitors are almost certainly underusing online PR and social media, so it's up to you to figure out a path that helps you grow. Don't wait for things to be perfect before you start, and remember: in the land of the blind, the one eyed man is king. Any time you are doing something better than your competitors, keep doing it. Your efforts in building your business' online profile could well be the most important thing you do for your business this decade.

Why Small Businesses Need a PR Strategy More Than Everyone Else

Think that you're too small to need a PR strategy? Think again. *Every company* has a public image which reflects what people think about them and why people choose to do business with them. The difference between a company with a PR strategy and one that doesn't is that the PR-savvy company is able to influence its public image in a way that is beneficial, while the passive company simply lets others dictate the conversation without putting forward their own voice.

This has always been true, but it has become *even more true* in the digital age. Not only does each company have an invisible public image which is made up of the fluffy thoughts, feelings, and views that consumers have about a company, but a company now also has a highly visible manifestation of their public image in the conversations that people are having about that company *publicly* online. Each Retweet, like and share, each star on Amazon, each testimonial left on your company's website, each blog post written about your products, represent a manifestation of your public image that the whole world has access to. While magazine coverage quickly became outdated and bad reviews were soon forgotten in the age of print, now bad reviews linger indefinitely in Google's archives, potentially haunting business owners months and years after the original reviewer had that one less-than-perfect interaction with your company.

Nowhere is this more apparent than with the arrival of review websites like tripadvisor.com. New restaurants and cafes literally live or die by their TripAdvisor reviews, with anything less than four stars essentially invisible to discerning customers looking for a place to eat. Almost the very first thing that a potential customer will do when deciding whether to do business with your company is Google your name, and their decision to buy, or not buy, will be hugely influenced by what they see that others have said online. When an 11–25 year old wants to know what kind of shoes or computer to buy, they don't look in newspapers and they certainly don't ask their parents – they ask Google instead.

Digital PR is the art of making sure that your customers only see good things when they put your name into a search engine.

How to Use this Book to Run a Totally Ninja Digital PR Campaign

If you are reading this book, you are either a small business owner looking to run their own digital PR campaign (we'll get to that later) or you are a marketing professional looking to add a new string to their bow. Or you're our mums (*hi mums!*).

Of course, we think that the best way to use this book is to read it cover to cover, back to front and sleep with it under you pillow (not forgetting to mention it to your friends online too), but we would say that – we wrote it. This book is designed to be all killer, no filler. If we don't think that it's useful or interesting to someone running their own business, we haven't included it. That being said, there are a number of people that will be reading this book more like a guide for DIY digital PR, and we've tried to make it as easy as possible for people to use it in that way too.

In this book we share what we've learnt about planning and doing Digital PR for businesses of all sizes. The goal is to give you everything you need to start using it for your business, even if you have no prior experience. To help you achieve this goal, we've included a number of *action points*. An action point is a simple, actionable instruction that you can carry out for your business or project. If you carry out all the action points listed on this book, then congratulations! You will be running your first ninja digital PR campaign.

Here's your first action point:

> **Action Point:** *Claim your free expert website and marketing review, complete with analysis of your competition and a tailored marketing plan to grow your business over the next 6–12 months.*

As a thank you for buying this book, we'd like to offer you a free review by one of our expert Review Ninjas, free of charge. We'll analyse your website, make recommendations about the sort of digital PR strategy that you can embark on, as well as doing some digging into what your competitors have been up to. Just fill in the short form on www.exposureninja.com/review and your review will be delivered to you by email in 2–3 working days.

Over the course of the book we're going to reference a lot of cool websites and tools that professional marketers and PR people use on a daily basis to run their own digital PR campaigns. For your convenience, we've listed all of these tools and websites at the end of the book, along with a brief introduction of how to use them. As the focus of this book is digital PR for small businesses with small budgets (for now), we've usually preferred the free tools to paid versions unless we think that the paid versions offer essential or irreplaceable features.

Why we Wrote this Book

Like all our books, this book is written for one reason: to help you make more money. Digital PR is a business activity and business activities can only be judged as successes or failures by their ability to make you more money than they cost. Digital PR returns on the investment by raising perceptions of your product or service, making it more visible and desirable in the eyes of your consumers. An additional benefit of digital PR can be found if you ever decide to sell your company – you'll find that buyers will pay an additional premium above and beyond the value of your assets if you've managed to build a brand name that consumers trust.

The pace of change is so fast it's almost frightening. While you used to be able to get any old website to the top of Google with some frankly ridiculous black hat search engine optimisation (SEO) tactics, Google's algorithms have become more sophisticated and now it takes time, planning, and carefully thought out maneuvers. Digital PR has become an increasingly important part of that maneuvering. While our clients used to want more SEO and just a little online PR, we're seeing a full reversal occur as Google continues to reward quality content above all else – and digital PR is the perfect breeding ground for the kind of content that Google loves.

One of the things that we're going to mention time and time again is the pace of change. Things are changing fast, so we've decided to laser-focus everything in this book for things that are best practice right now. Of course, we're constantly experimenting and developing new strategies too, so to keep you current with everything that's working we'll be updating this book. As a thank you for reading and supporting this book, head over to www.exposureninja.com/pr-book to make sure you receive free lifetime updates.

Chapter 1

Setting Goals for your Digital PR Campaign

Digital PR is a marketing activity, and marketing activities should be judged primarily on their ability to bring in a return on investment (ROI). Generally if something costs more money than it brings in, then it should be either tweaked or dropped. And yet, so few businesses really know whether their marketing activity is bringing them ROI or not. Why? *They just aren't tracking the figures.*

In this chapter:

- What does digital PR success look like? Reviewing the metrics of success
- Setting SMARTer goals
- Example goal #1: direct sales
- Example goal #2: become an authority figure in your field
- Example goal #3: gain influence, and a following, on social media
- Example goal #4: create an awesome email database & newsletter signups

Now admittedly some activities are easier to track than others. If you spend $500 promoting a product and you make a profit of $1,000 as a result, that's simple. But calculating the value that a social media campaign or a digital PR campaign adds to your business can be trickier. Still, too many business people throw their hands up at the first hurdle and say: "Well it looks kind of tricky so I won't even try." This is an attitude that is unacceptable in every other area of running a business, so it makes no sense to indulge it in here.

To this end, we're going to use this chapter to talk about:

1. Measuring the current success of your business
2. Identifying clear and achievable goals for your digital PR campaign
3. Measuring the success of your digital PR campaign, and making adjustments accordingly

If you set out to sea without any idea where you are going or how you are going to get there, it will likely be a very long time until you reach land again. The even more pertinent question to ask yourself is why you're going out there in the first place? Without knowing this, there's no guarantee that you'll reach that paradise island you dreamed of and even less of a guarantee that it's actually the place that you really want to be when you get there.

In the same way, your digital PR goals will map out your campaign and will let you know when you've successfully achieved at your final objective.

Different businesses should have different objectives. The aim of every business is to make money, but the best route to this goal will depend on the state that they are in. A multinational company might make the most money by expanding their existing product or service into a new market, but a small business might not even be known in their own hometown, let alone abroad.

If objectives are clearly outlined and measurable then they are much easier to achieve. A plan such as "be the best accountancy firm in my city" gets points for ambition, but falls flat because *best* is something that can be defined in multiple ways. Are we talking about being the firm that makes the most money, is best known, or delivers the best service here? The three aren't mutually exclusive but each requires a very different plan to achieve them.

The last important reason for having a plan is because it makes it much easier to reflect and make changes as you go along. Very few people get any marketing activity perfectly right first time around, but so long as you are measuring your targets you can see how or why you've drifted off course and take reasonable steps to get back on track. Doing more of what works and less of what doesn't is an admirable business strategy, but to be effective you need to have "working" and "not working" clearly defined for your business.

Reviewing the Metrics of Digital PR Success (Sales, Traffic, Keyword Rankings, Backlinks, Domain Authority, and Klout)

So let's look at various ways of measuring the success of your business's digital PR strategy. Many of the measures will be related to the success of your business's website, which is of particular focus for any digital PR campaign. If you haven't already done so, now would be a good time to get a free website review over at www.exposureninja.com/review.

1. Increasing Sales

There's one metric that any businesses can't fail to track and that's sales. Sales is the oxygen that keeps any business alive and is a perfectly good metric for tracking your digital PR success.. Sales results are also numbers that are fairly hard to argue with or misinterpret, though obviously it's important to identify which of your sales are the most profitable.

Remember that tracking sales, or any other metric, isn't simply a case of comparing your January numbers to your February numbers and attributing any increase (or lack thereof) to the digital PR campaign that started on February 1st. We're big fans of conversion tracking using analytics software such as Google Analytics, and by monitoring the proportion of your customers that came through PR links and through increased organic search traffic, you can far more accurately assign sales to your D-PR activity.

Does your business take sales calls by phone? Rather than having your sales team ask leads where they discovered you (this generally leads to fuzzy and incomplete results), consider using call tracking software to generate trackable numbers which give accurate data down to the outcome of the call.

If you've got a niche e-commerce property and your goal is to increase sales for example, a blogger outreach program that has high authority niche bloggers reviewing and running contests giving away your products can drive a lot of highly qualified and commercial traffic to your site, increasing sales of the products featured significantly. We'll look at blogger outreach in Chapter 7.

2. Generating Website Traffic

If your PR work isn't focussed on driving sales of a particular product or service, but rather raising awareness of your business as a whole, then website traffic can be a good measure of performance. A certain percentage of the visitors to your site will convert to customers (your website's **conversion rate**) and a certain percentage of visitors will click off of your website without taking any meaningful action (your website's **bounce rate**). Getting a lot of traffic is important, but it won't mean anything for your business if you have a low conversion rate or a high bounce rate, because these generally mean that either your website isn't up to scratch or the traffic you are generating isn't qualified.

As mentioned above, Google Analytics provides plenty of useful traffic data that you can use to measure progress. It's worth noting here that many of our clients who come to us complaining of a traffic problem ("not enough people are visiting my website") are actually suffering from a *conversion* problem (of the visitors that arrive, too few are sufficiently motivated to enquire or buy).

It's likely that everyone who is considering a digital PR campaign knows the importance of keyword ranking. If you rank highly in Google for a keyword like "buy nike trainers" then you are just a move or two away from an early retirement on a beautiful Mediterranean island. The most recent studies show that ranking in the top 'organic' (free) position will get you over 30% of the clicks from that search results page, so it's no surprise that prominent organic ranking is top of many marketers' priority lists.

A digital PR campaign is one of the most effective ways we've found to improve the ranking of any website, because it's a good way to attract *backlinks*. A stable of backlinks from respected websites is one of Google's three main ranking factors. This is because the internet is a lot like a popularity contest – and a backlink is just like being talked about. If you are being talked about (getting backlinks), then you must be popular. And if all the coolest kids are talking about you, then you must be one of the cool kids too! For more advice on improving your website's ranking, check out the book How To Get To The Top Of Google.

Perhaps more important than the *amount* of traffic you receive is the *type* of traffic you receive. As alluded to before, you are rewarded when visitors have meaningful engagements with your website and you get penalised when people bounce off it. This means that you really should be identifying what your main audience actually looks like and tailoring your marketing efforts accordingly. Are your biggest customers 18–24 year-old Asian men that went to university, have no children, and have an income of $150k+? Then you should be advertising in (or at least emulating) the Economist, a website that is most often read by people of the above description. One tool for audience analysis of this kind is quantcast.com.

While a good digital PR campaign will increase your website's traffic, a Ninja digital PR campaign will emphasise driving the right kind of traffic.

As an example, creating high quality infographics that get shared in the right places can be an extremely effective way to increase traffic as people share and repost them, funnelling more traffic to your site each time.

3. Building Authority

So far we have been thinking in terms of easily quantifiable stuff such as sales, traffic and ranking, but what about those concepts that are fluffier but no doubt business-defining, such as influence, trustworthiness and authority? These concepts have always existed in business. For as long as there have been traders, there have been traders that people trust and traders that are known to cheat. Traders that are known to have the best goods and traders that are known to have the worst goods stand out from the crowd. Until the digital age, this kind of knowledge was difficult to measure. But now that everyone is online and our conversations, emails, and interactions are stored in Google's archives and the NSA's databases, it is becoming possible to quantify previously intangible concepts such as authority.

One of the most useful tools for measuring a website's authority is **domain authority** (DA). Domain authority looks at a website's popularity, age, and size and gives you a number between one and a hundred. The most authoritative websites are scored highly, while less trustworthy sites get a lower score. The venerable BBC website has a DA of of 100, whereas www.shadyspamsite.ly might have a score of 10 or lower. Websites that have a higher DA tend to be more profitable than websites with a lower DA and will usually rank much higher..

A website's DA is not yet a measure that typical customers use knowingly, but users are more likely to buy from a high DA website as this score reflects website ranking on search engines as well as website quality and user-friendliness. A higher authority website is likely to be one of the first, good looking websites someone lands on when searching on Google. You can add a toolbar to your browser that lets you see a website's DA at a glance over at moz.com/tools/seo-toolbar.

We'll look at how to get your business covered in the media in Chapter 4 and you'll learn how it's possible to get your business featured in many of the highest authority sites online, piggybacking their authority in the process.

4. Exerting Influence

Influence is a key concept in public relations. The idea is simple: some people are particularly influential and these people set the trends that the rest of the world follow. Celebrities, be they TV stars like Kim Kardashian or the Twitter/YouTube stars like Zoella that are followed by hundreds of millions of under-twenty-year-olds, can catapult businesses to new levels of popularity with a Tweet, photo or video featuring one of their products. Top fashion bloggers can command $5,000–$25,000 just to feature a brand's product in one post; brands have been reportedly paying as much as $100,000–$300,000 to appear in Kylie Jenner's Instagram posts. The magnitude of these payments indicates the profit that this authority can generate, and if you're already clued in on the digital PR game, you might be either thinking of working with one of these influential people, or building the people within your brand up to be influencers.

Like authority, influence is a metric that can be measured. Your **Klout Score** is a number between one and a hundred that measures your ability to drive action across social media networks. Someone with a high Klout score, such as Justin Bieber (92), can drive people into a buying frenzy when they're shown wearing a particular jacket or trainers for instance. For more information about Klout, check out klout.com/corp/score.

The good news is that you don't need to be Tweeted by a Kardashian to profit from online influence and we'll be looking at how to identify the most suitable influencers for your business in Chapter 4.

5. Cultivating Brand Trust & Credibility

In order to get any traffic that comes to your website to convert to actual paying customers who are spending all their green ones on your products or services, you need to create a brand that people trust. We already touched on the fact that a higher authority website is more trustworthy because it is well established and already used by lots of other people.

Another way to build brand trust is through working with influencers and having them vouch for your brand on their blog or social media channels. People will quickly start thinking, "Well, if this this guy that I follow and trust recommends this product, then it must be good!" Essentially, you're piggybacking off the back of other people who are already trusted online.

Gaining product reviews is a particularly important aspect of building brand trust. How you go about gaining product reviews will depend on your business. E-commerce websites like Amazon and Argos have an on-site review section under each product listing where customers are able to leave reviews, and this also works well for new e-commerce websites. Local, often service-based businesses may look to Google Local listings or Facebook to collect reviews.

Off-site reviews are another option. These are reviews of your products or services that are written on other websites or blogs, usually including a link back to your business website. Many potential customers will search google with a phrase like "[product name] review" before making a final decision to purchase. By inviting prominent websites and blogs to review your products, you can make sure that these searches throw up highly authoritative reviews. Off-site reviews can be organised with bloggers through a blogger outreach strategy (we'll look at how that works later on).

Whether your business is new or established, being seen in high authority publications is a fast way to get credibility with your audience. If you're looking for a personal trainer, for example, and you have two choices. Would the fact that one of them has been featured in newspapers and interviewed live on national TV in front of millions of people sway your decision? What you'll find is that your conversion rates go up and you're able to sustain a higher price relative to your competitors, because being associated with this sort of authority has a hypnotic effect on buyers.

Now that we have the tools for measuring success at our disposal we can begin to set goals. This involves looking at where we are, where we want to be, and then identifying the correct strategy for our desired outcome.

Setting SMARTer goals

We've been consistently amazed at how poor most business owners are at setting goals for their marketing. Most business people don't really think about their long-term and short-term goals beyond "make more money by selling more stuff." If they do think about it a little more, it rarely gets further than "sell more of my *most expensive* stuff."

Setting goals needs to be smart, and we'll use the painful but effective SMART acronym to help us do it.

Specific: "Sell more stuff" is what all businesses want to do, but it is a terrible goal for a business because it is so unspecific. How exactly are we going to sell more stuff? Instead of "sell more stuff" we could have a goal that instead says "increase sales through my website by 50%."

Measurable: The next step is to make the goal measurable. What counts as success in this instance? An increase in traffic of one extra visitor is still an increase, but most would not call it a success. Instead, we can say "increase traffic to my website by 10%."

Agreed on: Here is where we come to the place where most people come unstuck. It's unlikely, unless you are still in the very early caffeine-infused days of your start-up, that there will be only one person involved in setting and completing a task. It's normally the work of a team or, at the very least, a manager who sets the task and an employee that carries it out. If you want your goal to be effective, it is essential that every single person involved understands and agrees to the goal. This is doubly important if you are outsourcing work. Make sure that the company that you are working with understands what your goal is and agrees that they will achieve it.

Realistic: This is an obvious one but it needs saying regardless: any goal set needs to be realistic otherwise it is at best pointless and at worst demotivating. We all want to be page one of Google as of immediately, but realistically these things take time. You want to hit that sweet spot where a goal is stretching but not demoralisingly impossible.

Time-bound: Perhaps most importantly of all, your goal must be attached to a time frame. From "increase traffic to my website by 10%" to "increase traffic to my website by 10% within the next 12 weeks." Set milestones and break longer tasks up into achievable sprints. If you haven't seen a 2.5% increase by the end of week three, then you may need to evaluate your strategy and check what's working and what isn't.

> **Action Point: Using the smart criteria outline above, set a goal for your first digital PR campaign**. *You can use any metric you like to measure your success, though the ones mentioned above (sales, keyword ranking, conversion rate, bounce rate, backlinks, DA, and klout) could be useful depending on your aim.*

Once you have your goal, it's time to think about the best way of setting out to achieve it! Picking the right strategy for your goal is something that takes years of practice to master. One thing is for sure – few people get it completely right first time. That's why it's important to break your goal up into distinct sprints and review and readjust at the end of each sprint according to your progress. To help you identify which method might work best for your particular goal, we've run through four different examples.

Example Goal #1: Direct Sales

The most obvious goal of all is increasing the amount of sales that you make from your website. First of all, you're going to need to calculate your current sales (a number you should be holding close to your heart!) as well as your projected sales. Remember to factor in seasonal changes that might affect your business, such as Christmas shopping. Then you need to set a realistic target and a timeframe for achieving that target by.

Your sales figure will be broadly driven by two different components: 1) the amount of people visiting your website (your traffic) and 2) the number of visitors that convert into customers (your conversion rate). Both components are important. A website with lots of traffic but no conversions is most likely unprofitable, and the same applies to a website with a high conversion rate but only a small handful of visitors. Broadly speaking, a website with high ticket items can get away with (and even expect) a lower conversion rate, as people need more time to decide that they want to spend a significant amount of money. The opposite is true for low ticket items.

While digital PR has a role to play in increasing your conversion rate through adding value to your product or service, optimising your website for conversion (removing barriers to sales and positioning your products in an attractive way) can help you unlock hidden profit from your existing website traffic.

Where digital PR really excels is in driving *more* traffic to your website. Ways to do this will differ depending on your circumstances, but it will probably include the following: creating valuable and keyword-rich content on your website, using paid advertising, getting featured in relevant publications, using blogger outreach, and using an engaging social media campaign. A key metric that will determine the amount of traffic that your website gets will be your **keyword ranking**, so take some time to determine which keywords are most relevant for your business (that you can compete on). If you need some help identifying suitable keywords, then we suggest claiming your free website review from www.exposureninja.com/review.

Example Goal #2: Become an Authority Figure in your Field

More subtle than directly selling your product to as many people as possible, is being seen as an authority in your industry. This is a goal that is just as applicable to small businesses as it is to large ones, and one of the key mistakes we see small businesses making is undervaluing their knowledge. You might think that something in your industry is obvious because it has become second nature to you, but that doesn't mean that it's obvious to your customers. In all likelihood your market is craving an expert who takes it upon themselves to educate the masses and build their credibility at the same time. Think of TV personalities who have side businesses offering the exact services they're known as experts for. This is no accident, and they're not usually doing it for the fame – they are using their public visibility to build their authority in their field.

To measure your influence and authority online, we're going to be looking to improve your domain authority. DA is calculated by three factors: your website's age, size, and popularity. Not a lot can be done about age other than getting your website online as soon as possible if it isn't already! Size, on the other hand, can be achieved by creating engaging web pages for your different product and service categories. Remember that while people like pictures, Google is still better at reading text than images, so to appeal to both we're going to include a decent mix of the two. Everything should be original, clear, and engaging – duplicating content simply to create a bigger website will most likely earn you both an indirect Google penalty and a high bounce rate.

To improve the popularity of your website we're going to want to build high quality links to your website (links are a hugely important way that Google and Moz calculate popularity). The best way to build quality links is to write engaging articles and get them placed in publications that are read by your target audience, along with an all-important link back to your website. This establishes you as an authority figure both in the eyes of your readers and Google.

It's worth pointing out that DA is just a unit of measurement, but it's one that is increasingly accurate and being used as standard across the industry. It's a simplified version of what Google measures when it's deciding on the authority of a website. However, while Google's ranking algorithms are top-secret and the source of endless speculation, DA is transparent and therefore a useful tool. DA is determined by taking a snapshot of your website, rather than an exhaustive index, so don't become obsessed by it, but it's certainly a useful indicator.

Example Goal #3: Build your Website's Blog into an Awesome Resource that Attracts Traffic and Converts

There are a whole bunch of reasons why you should include a blog on your business's website, and if you don't do it you're bananas. Most importantly it's your soapbox where you share content for your social media channels and to build links to. It can build up a brand image of your company or you personally, as well as attracting more potential customers to your website. Then of course you have the SEO benefits: it gives search engines more text content to crawl and more pages to rank.

What we see all too often is random, undernourished content on whatever topic has come to mind thrown for the sake of just getting new content on-site. Someone has on their to do list "write a blog" each month, and they do this with the enthusiasm of a child doing their homework whilst friends play outside on a summer's evening. Building a blog can be an incredible tool for maximising your reach, keeping potential customers on your website and making conversions, so for it to feel a chore is a chronic waste and a sign of a lack of strategy.

There are various measures to determine the impact of your blog, such as the amount of traffic coming to blog pages, the number of blog subscribers or newsletter signups, the clickthroughs to products pages on your website, the number of social media shares that your blog posts garner, and so on. To build your blog into an incredible resource that answers all the questions your target customers might have, and to use it as a means of converting new customers, you could set a goal along the lines of "gain x new leads from my blog each month by producing and promoting y amount of content."

When we're working on client campaigns, we'll usually write a blog post or series of posts around a certain topic whilst we are doing outreach to promote articles about that subject. To be able to show publishers an example of our writing on that subject or a close variant is useful, and is relatively low effort because we've already taken the time to do the research and formulate an opinion on the topic.

Example Goal #4: Gain Followers and Influence Them (on Social Media)

Social media is, generally speaking, not the place to make direct sales, but it is the place to engage with your customers and even make some of them into living, breathing, Tweeting, liking, sharing spokespeople for your service or products. Social media comes with its own wide range of metrics that you can use when setting goals – perhaps you want to reach a certain number of followers, likes or shares.

As mentioned above, Klout is a good tool to use if you want to focus on one metric that tracks your progress across multiple networks. It also measures engagement rather than activity which is very important in social media. Both Twitter and Facebook increase the visibility of profiles that attract engagement and decrease the visibility of profiles that don't get any responses, creating a virtuous cycle for engaging profiles and a vicious one for those that are seen to be spammy. You might have noticed that if you write some overly self promotional posts for Facebook that get relatively little attention from your audience, subsequent posts have significantly less visibility. Meanwhile if you share content on your pages that has proven viral spread, you'll notice that the odd self promotional post gets *significantly* more reach.

An example of an influence-related goal might be "improve my Klout score from x to y by future date". You'd go about achieving that goal by creating compelling social media profiles on the platforms that are used by your customers and creating content that is likely to be shared, liked, and Retweeted (i.e. probably not just pictures of your product and invitations to "check out our website"). You could write a whole book on the intricacies of social media marketing and we have, it's called Profitable Social Media Marketing and you should read it if your digital PR campaign hinges on successful social media. As always, regularly review so that you can do more of what works and less of what doesn't.

Example Goal #5: Create an Awesome Email Database

The vast majority of underperforming websites have only one goal in mind: make the sale. If the visitor is not ready to buy *right now*, there is little for them to do but wander in, have a look around and wander off.

The highest performing websites will often segment their visitors into multiple levels of 'willingness to buy'. Those who are ready to buy right now can do so, but those who are in the research phase, curious or just killing time are catered for too. By offering lead generation 'bait' such as a free guide, sample or some other tasty tidbit, high converting sites collect the names and email addresses of people who, whilst they're not ready to buy now, might be ready to buy in the future.

Creating this type of email database of existing and potential customers to market to (email marketing) is something that every business will need to do at some stage and most of them will say to themselves, "I wish I had started doing this earlier! It would have made life so much easier!" Make life easy for yourself, and start doing this now if you haven't done so already. Collecting emails is useful on a number of levels, but the key reason is that it is a relatively easy way of retargeting old or potential customers that at one stage were interested in your business.

The goal is clear, get a certain amount of customers to sign up to your newsletter, or simply get a certain amount of emails in your database for use at a later date. The methods for achieving this goal vary, but generally you have to think in terms of "what's in it for them?" We all strive for an empty inbox, so I have to be getting something of value if I'm going to give a company my email address, and 'sign up for our newsletter' has about as much appeal as a 5am telesales call). One of the most effective lead generation baits we've found is a giveaway. Run a competition and give your most sought after products away to a couple of lucky winners in exchange for the email addresses of everyone who takes part (and don't forget to include social media too). You can use a simple software such as rafflecopter.com to get a competition live and online in a matter of minutes (more on this later).

If giving away products isn't relevant or is too expensive this early on, you can give away information instead. If you run a HR software, for instance, you can invite people to attend webinars on popular topics related to HR software. Collect the email addresses of those that sign up in exchange for a free place at the event.

Chapter 2

How to Use Content Marketing in Your Digital PR Campaign

Content marketing is an unmissable element of any complete digital PR strategy, so much so that it has become hard to distinguish where the hyperbole ends and where the, well, actual *content* begins. But while many have trumpeted content marketing as a unique product of the internet age, we're going to see that content marketing actually has a history nearly as long as marketing itself.

Content is, essentially, anything that enables you to communicate with your customers. Writing an article, creating an infographic, composing a Tweet or animating a video – these are all examples of content creation because they all contain some kind of message or idea that is passed from the creator of the content to the consumer. Content marketing is creating and promoting content that is specifically designed to help your business achieve its marketing goals.

In this chapter:

- What is Content Marketing?
- What Successful Content Marketing Looks Like
- What is an Advertorial?
- What About Press Releases?
- How to Come up with Ideas for Content
- Tools for Researching Topics and Trends

1. What is Content Marketing?

Content marketing is a very simple concept. Basically we're looking to sneak a promotional message into our audience's brains via something that they *really* want to consume. Newspaper advertorials are a precursor to content marketing as we know it today, and it's no accident that in many cases they vastly outperform traditional ads. People read newspapers for the articles not the ads, after all. And if it looks like an article, smells like an article, then it's going to get read.

One of the clearest online examples of content creation is the email newsletter. You, the content creator, have a message that you want to communicate to your audience. Your message is how fantastic your new product is. To convey your message to your audience, you write a newsletter telling everyone exactly how groundbreaking your new product is. Your newsletter is the content, and because you are using your newsletter to achieve your company's goals, sending your newsletter out to your email database is content marketing. Simple, right?

The key with content marketing, as with all advertising, is to make the content bit as compelling as possible. If you've ever read a typical corporate press release announcing a product launch for example, this is basically the antithesis of what we're aiming for: a dry, dull and purely self promotional piece of little to zero interest to most ordinary people.

Going back to our email newsletter, because your audience has their finger hovering over the DELETE button as they read, your newsletter must offer something of value to your readers – otherwise they won't read it. This value could be information, entertainment, some kind of discount or gift, *but it has to exist alongside your content's original message if your content marketing is going to be seen by anyone*. While adverts are just placed next to something of value in order to be seen by the viewer, the commercial message in content marketing is *built in* so as to be indistinguishable from the content.

Let's sum up the differences between content marketing and advertising:

	Contains a message?	Helps achieve marketing objectives?	Contains something of value for the audience?	Is paid for?
Advertising	Yes.	Yes.	Not necessarily.	Yes.
Content marketing	Yes.	Yes.	Yes.	Not necessarily.

2. What Successful Content Marketing Looks Like (Robots in Disguise)

Content marketing is not a new phenomenon. In fact, it's much older than many people realise. In 1984, Hasbro, a toy manufacturer, thought of a relatively new way of selling their action figures. Instead of creating a twenty second commercial that talks about how awesome their new action toys were, they decided to create a twenty minute TV show that showed their audience exactly how awesome their new action toys were. The show was a sensational hit, and Transformer-related toys flew off the shelves at an astounding rate. In fact, Transformers has become so entrenched in modern popular culture that many people don't realise that Optimus Prime and the gang started out as content marketing in disguise.

But while Hasbro taught the world a valuable lesson about content marketing in 1984, content marketing has had a real renaissance in the internet age. This is because of two crucial factors:

1. The internet connects businesses to a potential audience of millions
2. The internet makes content creation *much cheaper* than ever before

Very few businesses have the resources to go out and create a TV show Hasbro-style just to promote their product. But by using resources that are free online, almost every business on the planet is able to start producing excellent content, such as blogs, infographics, or podcasts. One of the key reasons that content marketing is such an excellent tool for small businesses is that it costs *as little* or *as much* as you want to spend on it. Let's look at some examples of super successful ninja content marketing from the internet age.

McDonald's: Our Food, Your Questions

McDonald's is a controversial brand that is admired in advertising circles perhaps just as much as it is hated in health circles. In fact, they intentionally exploited their less than stellar reputation in their "our food, your questions" content marketing campaign. What they did was invite their audience to post their questions online and committed to answering all of them. As you can imagine, not all of the questions were particularly polite, but McDonald's went out of their way to answer the questions in a kind and humorous (if slightly obsequious) way.

This is a stroke of evil genius. It gave lots of people the opportunity to interact with the McDonald's brand. By posting a question and getting a response, McDonald's immediately feels less like a faceless corporation and more like a group of people, and people tend to like people. But if that weren't reason enough to run the campaign, the second reason is what earned it the reputation for being "the greatest example of content marketing ever."

Larry B. went ahead and asked what many people were surely thinking: "Is your meat made out of cardboard?" Rather than censor the post, McDonald's went ahead and answered it: "Absolutely not. We don't think cardboard would taste very good in our burgers." Now Larry B. is far from the first person to wonder if McDonald's meat is made from cardboard. But now that McDonald's answered the question themselves online, *every other person that Googles the same question will be directed to the McDonald's official answer* rather than some snarky McDonald's hating forum. They stopped hundreds of McDonald's rumours dead in their tracks by giving an answer to every single one of them.

Colgate: Oral and Dental Resource Center

You don't have to have a cool or interesting product to create some absolutely out of this world content. While McDonald's showed us how to get engagement, Colgate demonstrates how to become the number one authority in your field with their massive oral and dental resource center. The website is nothing less than an encyclopedia on every single tooth-related issue that you can possibly imagine, covered in an accurate and informative tone. Try asking Google a question about dentistry and I'll bet you that Colgate comes in on the first page.

Racking Inspection Training Company: Dominating Google News

One of our major success stories was the digital PR campaign we've run for a small business who provide racking inspection trainings for warehouses. Have you ever heard of a more dry subject matter? Probably not, but it doesn't matter. There are only a few experts in the world of racking inspection training and even fewer who are writing about it, which means we made sure these guys were absolutely dominating their market.

We write around a dozen articles each month relating to racking inspections and health and safety more broadly. Some are published on the company's own blog, and others are published on websites in the workplace health and safety niche. If you type "racking inspection training" into Google News and you can bet your pound sterling than half of the articles on that first page are written by our client. After just 4 months of our SEO and digital PR work, the company's website was on page one of Google for 21 of their target keywords and in the top three results on Google for 8 of their target keywords. Pretty ninja for a small business.

Paintballing Company: Featured on the World's Largest Paintball Forum

When it comes to paintballing, there are only a limited number of publications in this niche but a whole load of companies competing for the Google top spots. We scoured the web for publications but quickly realised that all of the paintball enthusiasts aren't just reading magazines, they're actively participating on paintball forums and engaging in conversations about paintballing techniques and strategies.

We got an article written by our team and the company owner picked up and published on PB Nation, the world's largest paintball forum. The forum users loved it. Within just 2 days, there were two pages of comments from paintball enthusiasts praising the advice in the article and adding to the discussion with their own tips.

3. What is an Advertorial?

There are few types of content marketing that are as contentious as advertorials. An advertorial is an advert that is placed in a magazine that mimics the style and appearance of an editorial. They are also known as 'native advertising' because the adverts look native to the publication they are in. The effect is that the reader usually gets halfway through the advertorial before realising that what they're reading is actually an ad.

But just because they annoy readers doesn't mean that they don't work. Jingles are infuriating but undoubtedly shift products and the same is true of advertorials – AB testing shows that advertorials attract 81% more orders than ads with identical copy in a traditional format, and they are a mindblowing five hundred times more likely to be read. The key to retaining goodwill with an advertorial is to make sure that the piece provides value as well as a pitch. Hollow advertorials that 'bait and switch' (setting up the article to be interesting but ultimately becoming a pure pitchfest) annoy people but it doesn't have to be like that!

4. What about Press Releases?

In the old days, it seemed like PR agencies did nothing but put together a never-ending stream of press releases communicating every possible facet of a business to the outside world. Digital PR has come a long way since then and content marketing strategies have evolved massively. Nowadays press releases are certainly less popular than they were and many companies are thinking about giving up on them altogether.

A press release is a message that a business sends to the press in the hopes that they will pick up the story and publicise it. The problem is that journalists are inundated with press releases from every kind of business imaginable – to the point where a full 50% of journalists say that they don't even read any of the press releases that they get from startups and small businesses anymore.

To maximise your chances of securing successful press in this harsh environment, you have to make sure that you have a newsworthy story (i.e. it is actually new, interesting, and would appeal to a broad array of readers). If you don't have a good story, shelve press releases and move on. Only once you have a story that your friends agree is genuinely interesting, then you can think about using press releases in your digital PR strategy.

The next step is crafting a killer headline for your press release. Remember, you've already lost 50% of the journalists that you've contacted, and unless your headline is exceptionally compelling you are about to lose the other 50%. The same applies to your subject line. Think of the first line of your actual email as an extension of your headline, the aim is to keep building the hype train and strike that delicate balance between raising the reader's curiosity and providing enough information so it's clear what you are talking about and why.

Next comes the actual body of the press release which should outline the story idea in under five hundred words. Keep reminding yourself that journalists are extremely busy people and will delete your email at a moment's notice if it starts to bore them. Do tailor your emails slightly to each publication, and do paste your press release into the body of your email rather than attach it to your email (you think journalists have time to open attachments!) Given how difficult it is to get a press release picked up and the amount of effort that goes into making one, it's fair to ask whether they are actually a good use of time. The answer is: only if they get picked up, which doesn't happen very often.

Here are two examples of the kind of thing that is worth writing a press release about:

Breast Milk Ice Cream

It's got breasts in the title and it makes people go "eurgh" or possibly "hmm" – an instant winner. A restaurant in Covent Garden got national coverage when it announced to the world that it was selling ice cream made from human breast milk, and it even went so far as to name the donor who would be providing the milk. The story did even better than usual because the restaurant tied the announcement to the debate that was going on at the time about public breast feeding. He also came up with a name for the ice cream that the Sun would be proud of: Baby Gaga.

It's sad but true: any story about breasts, or anything that makes people go "yuck" is more likely to be a hit, but there has to be a genuine connection to your business too.

Paintball Bullet Tester

A paintballing company got an enormous amount of coverage when it announced that it was looking to hire a bullet tester with a high tolerance for pain. The company put up job ads on all the big jobs sites, describing the exact kind of stamina and endurance needed by candidates. Humour is the key ingredient here, with a healthy dose of curiosity mixed in. Whether a bullet tester ever actually got hired, who knows, but it sure got some publicity for the paintball company.

How does your story compare to breast milk ice cream or paintball bullet tester? "New accountancy firm in Milton Keynes" simply isn't going to cut the mustard. Only devote the time to crafting a press release and sending the necessary hundreds of emails once you actually have something worth sharing. Otherwise, don't waste your time.

The other route to go down is submitting your story to press release websites. Since Google's algorithmic changes to Panda, the link benefit of these are marginal at best and actually harmful at worst. Again, with these websites it's probably only worth doing if you have a press release that people are actually going to share. Once you do have that story, consider checking out the following free websites:

ResponseSource.com
PRLog.org
PR.com
PR-Inside.com
i-Newswire.com
OnlinePRNews.com

These are two of the best paid websites:

PRNewswire.com
PRWeb.com

5. Choosing the Right Form of Content Marketing for Your Target Audience

As you may have noticed, content marketing can take many different forms. Articles, blogs, social media engagement, books, podcasts, press releases, email newsletters, advertorials, and videos are just some examples of the different forms that content marketing can take. Understanding which form of content marketing will work best for your business is an essential aspect of any coherent digital PR strategy.

Just as Transformers is a cartoon perfectly geared towards the people who are most likely to buy the Transformers toys (children), you must choose the type of content that is most likely to be consumed by your ideal customer. But before we can decide which content is right for your customer, you first have to identify your customer.

Chapter 3

Identifying your Target Market & Building a Tailored Digital PR Strategy

You can't just create a heap of content and hope it will be a success. You have to know who you are creating it for and why they will consume it. It's a very simple concept: you can't hit the bullseye if you don't know where the dartboard is.

In this chapter:

- *How to Identify Your Target Audience*
- *Building a Persona*
- *Appealing to Your Target Audience*
- *What Kind of Digital PR Turns Your Audience On?*

Taste is subjective. What appeals to one person repels another. Faced with the natural variations in taste present in society, marketers must think very carefully about how to use their resources. Casting a wide net is expensive, and it pulls up all kinds of crap, but putting the *right net* in the *right place* at the *right time* nets you the exact results you were looking for at a fraction of the cost. But before you can design your net, first you must identify the characteristics of your fish.

Very few businesses have a product or service that is bought by everyone. Even something as universal as a toothbrush is significantly more likely to be bought by one section of society (mums) than another (their teenage sons).

If you have enough money to buy one billboard to advertise your luxury brand of alkaline mineral water, where do you put it? Kensington or Croydon?

Is your new range of organic, fair trade, maca-infused, cacao nib nibbles going to be better placed in Waitrose or Asda?

While there are always individuals that defy categorisation, and while demographics are starting to feel less fixed than ever before, target marketing remains an essential tool for the savvy marketer.

How to Identify Your Target Audience

Take a look at what your business is selling and then begin to think about who you want to sell it to – even better, do this the other way round and think about what the people you're selling to need and start selling that. You should aim to answer *at least* the following six questions about your target audience:

1. How old are they?
2. Where do they live?
3. What gender are they?
4. What is their education status?
5. What ethnicity are they?
6. What's their income (buying power)?

Moving through the buckets, sex, age, income – eventually you reach a person that both *wants to buy* and *is able to buy*.

These factors are important because a fifteen-year-old Asian girl from Birmingham consumes content in a totally different way to a fifty-eight-year-old male pensioner from Lancashire. Once you've answered these questions you can start to construct an avatar. An avatar is a representation of your target customer. The more details you fill in about your avatar, the more that you can start understanding the way they are likely to behave. This means that you can tailor the content that you create to the type of target customer that you are hoping to attract.

To give a clear example, the latest statistics show that teenagers (twelve to seventeen) watch less TV than any other age group. Between 2011 and 2015 there was a 30% contraction in the number of hours of TV watched by teenagers. Where are they all going? They are migrating away from traditional forms of media and towards online video sites such as YouTube. To the twelve

to seventeen year-old age group, even Facebook has become uncool as their parents and grandparents have started to understand and regularly use their Facebook profile. This group prefers the supposed anonymity of Snapchat that makes it harder for parents to keep track of what they're doing...
What does this all mean for businesses? It means that if your primary audience is twelve to seventeen year-olds then TV ads and even Facebook ads might not be the way to go. You need to come to the place that your target audience is already at if you want to get their attention. Try making some hilarious YouTube videos, getting coverage from bloggers, or even running a social media campaign on Snapchat if you want to see real results here.

Action Point: Sketch out a persona for your target customer. *I know that this might sound a bit like a primary school activity for creating a storybook character, but trust me, this is an essential part of understanding who you're trying to sell to. Without it, you risk losing your focus and targeting too broad of an audience.*

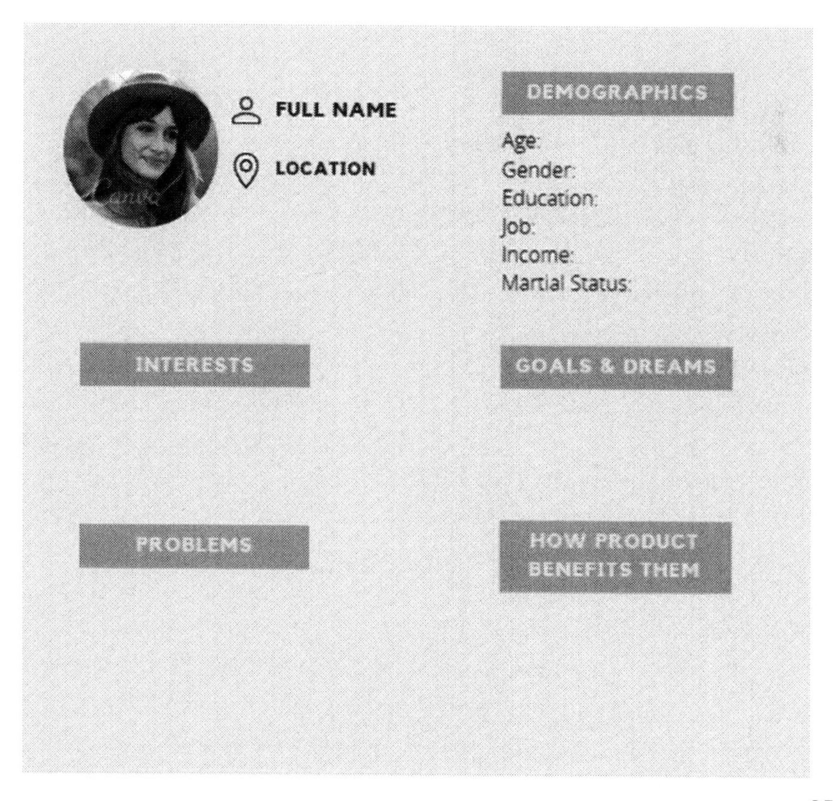

Let's take a look at how audience identification feeds in digital PR strategy. Let's say you run a dental clinic in London and you specialise in cosmetic dentistry procedures – teeth whitening, straightening and so on. You want to target your business to customers with a good income who are concerned about their appearance and oral health, which will likely lead you to focus on young professionals in their late twenties and early thirties.

They want information about what cosmetic dentistry options are available for them and the costs, so you produce marketing materials and a **content strategy** around this.

You can further use this information for **targeted keyword discovery**. This means researching keywords based on what your target audience wants, not just on the content that you already have on your website. Our cosmetic dentist can look at what their audience wants (i.e. cosmetic dental treatments), research keywords relating to this and optimise their website accordingly. Knowing a young professional may be interested in teeth whitening or invisible braces means it's easier to determine top keywords in this niche and use them to gain visibility for specific areas of your website.

DIY Market Research

To find out exactly which of your services pique your target customers' interest, it may be worth undertaking some **DIY market research**. If you're starting up a new coffee shop, for example, why not head down the road and spend a few hours in a competitor's coffee shop? Spend some time finding out what each customer orders: Do they just get a drink or food as well? What products are most popular? Do they prefer to stay in or takeaway? When are the busiest periods? You can use all of this to find trends and predict preferences of your own customers.

If market research for your product isn't as straightforward as spending time at a similar business, consider conducting focus groups for marketing research. If you can gather a group of people who are your target demographic, then you can run one on your own. If not, you may consider using a professional market research company.

If you're running an online e-commerce business or similar, then check out website's of your competitors. What products are featured on their homepage? Which ones are they pushing in sales? What are they sharing on their social media accounts? Can you find any customer reviews of their products?

What's their unique selling point (USP)? Compare this to your own website and consider running a **user test** through a service like **Peek User Testing** to see how the average internet user responds to your website's design and calls to action (CTA).

If you have already built the beginnings of a customer base, look at your current data. Which of your webpages are people landing on most often? What terms have they searched before landing on your website? Which items are your top sellers, and which are less popular? You can also conduct surveys of your current audience by using on-site surveys or using websites such as SurveyMonkey to find out which products they like and don't like, their thoughts on pricing, and what attracts them to your website.

Building a Digital PR Strategy for Your Target Audience

When deciding the focus of your business' digital PR strategy, it's not simply a case of picking the ideas that you like the most or the strategy that will be easiest to accomplish. You want to appeal to your audience, and they want to know you care about them and will solve their problem. There are many factors that need to be fed in to make sure your strategy appeals to your target consumers and is also achievable for a business of your size and stature.

You should consider the following before making any decisions about a digital PR strategy:

- What are your main business objectives and how can digital PR support them?
- What will appeal to your target audience? Where do they spend their time online? What are they into? What are they reading? Who do they follow?
- What is your unique selling point (USP), and how does that influence your digital PR?
- What is your budget? What are your realistic digital PR options?
- What are the giants in your industry doing? What can you learn from them?
- What are your competitors doing? If they're doing nothing, then sweet! You'll soon outrank them. If they're doing stuff, how can you do it better?

All of the content that you produce during your digital PR and content marketing activities, whether it's advice articles, how-to guides, blogs, newsletters, infographics, videos, social media posts, needs to appeal to your target audience. Plan your content types carefully and provide information backing up why this content will appeal to your audience. Be as specific as you can in your reasoning. Sure, there will be an element of trial and error, but the more information you can start off with the better your chances of success are.

Chapter 4

Researching Content Ideas & Getting in the Media

So you've decided to try your hand at content marketing and identified your target audience. Now what? Coming up with the ideas for your digital PR strategy and getting them in front of the right eyes is what it's all about – but it's not easy. Fortunately we're here to prevent the panic you might be experiencing right now and guide you through the process of coming up with ideas, creating content, and getting it in the media.

In this chapter:

- Tips for Finding Ideas for Your Content
- Hosting Your Own Content vs Guest Posting Elsewhere
- What's Wrong with Duplicate Content?
- Compiling a List of Target Publications
- How to Tell a Good Website from a Spammy One
- Getting into Niche, Industry-Specific and Up-and-Coming Publications
- Getting into the National Newspapers
- How to Pitch to Editors: Finding Contact Details & Creating a Press List
- Writing the Perfect Pitch
- Networking & Follow Up Articles

Tips for Finding Ideas for Your Content

Few things in life are more terrifying than a blank page, but this is a hurdle that you can't afford to stumble at now. Remember that content creation isn't easy and that other businesses struggle at least as much as you do. Take heart in the fact that many more people will give up at the blank page stage, making your success even more valuable for being the exception rather than the rule.

Why Written Content?

There are too many different possible content formats for us to cover in a meaningful way in this book, so we're going to focus on written content for this rest of the chapter. Not only is written content the most accessible type of content for small business owners to create, but it is also the case that long-form written content is more likely to be shared than shorter content, and that people tend to engage more with written content than they do with other kinds of content. The process for coming up with the content ideas which we will discuss works with other formats too, though there will be some minor adjustments.

Setting Goals and Parameters

Just as you should have a goal for your overall digital PR strategy, you should also have a goal for each individual piece of content that you create. This can be a simple goal, such as explaining a particular concept really well, or achieving a certain number of page views or shares. It could also be a more ambitious goal, such as securing a particular client or getting your article shared by a particular influencer that you have identified.

Along with goals also come parameters. You need to decide what you want to get out of your content, and then assign parameters accordingly. Time is money, so if you are short on time then you need to set a reasonable limit on how long you will dedicate to each piece. Likewise you could set budgetary limits according to how much cash you have to play with. Also, bear in mind other limits such as access to skills and technology.

Finding Inspiration in a Swipe File — Write What You Like

Now is the time to go looking for inspiration, and what better place to start than with the things that inspire you? Start by browsing the websites that you like and give you an emotional reaction. Analyse how they achieve these effects and whether they could be applicable to your business and to your format of content creation.

Save ideas that you like into a swipe file that you can browse when coming up with new ideas. You can bookmark webpages that you think do something really well, or you can save them using software like **Evernote** or websites such as **Trello Board** and **Pinterest.**

Write for Your Audience

Alternatively, if you are not very similar to the target audience that you have identified, you are going to have to start thinking out of the box. Instead of visiting websites that you like, start visiting websites that *they like* and note down common themes and concerns. What is getting a response and what is falling flat? For each piece of content you create, you should be able to explain who the target audience is and why they are going to engage with it.

Stay on Trend

Trends are an incredibly important phenomenon that content creators must be aware of. By catching trends early you can gain massive exposure for your business, by jumping on a trend too late you can be seen as an imitator, outdated, or worst of all, boring. To understand what's trending you'll need to use a tool like **Google Trends** which shows the search volume for keywords. This allows you to compare different trends and identify the words that people are using to discuss current events.

CASE STUDY: A LOCAL PERSONAL TRAINER GETS ON NATIONAL TELEVISION
Being on trend can multiply the effects of your digital PR campaign enormously. We were able to use Google Trends to identify a key fitness trend for one of our clients, a local personal trainer. We then helped him to create written content covering the trend (which was waist training) and had that published as a guest blog on a reasonably popular website. From there, the article was picked up by a number of newspapers and our personal trainer was even asked onto the BBC to discuss the trend, live on air!

Pay Attention to the News

Related to being on trend is being topical. Responding to news stories and current events is an excellent way to add something of value to the conversation before anyone else gets there. Is a new law being proposed? Talk loudly about how that law will affect your business – people may not have considered your side of the story yet and it could well inform the debate. You can use the **Google News** tab to search for recently published news stories.

If you really have an opinion on a news piece that you've seen online, especially on a big news site like the Guardian, the Telegraph, the Daily Mail and so on, then write a letter to the editor with your opinion about it. Remember to tell them who you are and why your opinion is valuable in this debate.

Competitor Analysis — if it worked for them it could work for you

All's fair in love and business. The industry leaders of your field have no doubt spent an enormous amount of time and effort determining what kind of ideas work well for content creation in your field and there's absolutely nothing from stopping you from looking at what they are doing and doing it better than them.

Tools like **Moz's Open Site Explorer** and **Backlink Watch** allow you to see what websites your competitor is getting backlinks from. Articles that are very successful tend to have more backlinks, so you should take note of articles that are getting a lot of links and try to determine how you could use similar techniques yourself. Using a tool like **Followerwonk** lets you to do a similar thing with Twitter, enabling you to see what techniques the market leaders are using to get engagement.

Competitor analysis is never about mindless imitation though. Just doing the same thing as other people will always leave you one step behind the crowd. Don't just try to do what has worked for someone else, try and work out *why* something worked for something else then use that knowledge in your own content creation.

Follow Journalists Closely

If you are following key journalists in your field on Twitter (and you should be) pay close attention to their conversations. If they start showing interest in a particular subject, asking questions or obviously doing research for an article, now might be a very good time to send them a Tweet or even to write an article of your own on the subject!

Journalists are very in-tune with what's hot or not, so pay attention to their signals and perhaps even beat them to the prize! A tool like **Response Source** allows journalists to do research by putting them in touch with PR people. The Twitter hashtag #JournoRequest is used for a similar purpose though is less strictly monitored. If you see a journalist for a high profile publication asking questions about a topic, it's likely that an article on the subject is imminent.

Picking the Best Idea

Once you have these ideas from various sources assembled in your swipe file and down on the obligatory brainstorm, how do you choose the best ones? First things first, return to your goals and parameters and cross out anything that isn't helping you achieve your aims or falls outside of the limits that you set yourself. Next, cross off anything that is even remotely boring. Once you are left with only the creme de la creme, get feedback from the people around you on what works and what doesn't. Once you have a concensus, you know that you have a winner, and the task of content creation can begin...

Tools for Researching Topics and Trends

We've mentioned a lot of different tools in this chapter, so we've made a list of our favourite tools and how you can use them for researching content ideas. **Buzzsumo:** a website that reveals what articles were written and how often they were read and shared. The free version gives you a very limited experience, but may be suitable for businesses that are just getting started with content creation. **Google Trends:** allows you to see how often a set of keywords are Googled, enabling you to see what is trending and how that trend has changed over time. It also predicts how the trend may change in the future, and you can compare different keyword sets to one another. This resource is excellent and free.

Google News: selecting 'news' on Google will filter your results to just show you what the newspapers are talking about. You can use this in conjunction with a Google alert to find out when your industry is being talked about and what people are saying.

Twitter: the social media site that is head and shoulders above the rest when it comes to up-to-the-minute news stories. Not only can you see what is trending, but you can also use Twitter to keep tabs on key influencers and journalists for your industry and even network with them.

Evernote: keep all of your content ideas in one easy place with this piece of software.

Trello Board: an interesting option for arranging content ideas onto a board and sharing that board with your colleagues.

Pinterest: social media site that lets you pin images. Use this website to pin images that inspire you and could be used as a springboard for your own content ideas at a later date.

Response Source: a paid-for enquiry service for journalists and PR people. Used by all the major national newspapers in the UK. Use it to get your ideas out there and to find new ideas that are being talked about by other people. Worth the money only for companies that are seriously dedicated to PR.

Open Site Explorer: another tool from Moz that allows you to learn more about a given website, particularly the number of backlinks that they have and where they are from. As mentioned above, you can analyse your competitor's links to see what topics are being shared.

Backlink Watch: similar to Moz, but always free and useful because it gives slightly different results. Behind the spammy-looking exterior is a useful piece of kit!

Getting your Business Covered by the Media

Let's say that you run a company that outsources HR services to other small and medium-sized businesses. The benefit is that you can provide HR services at a lower cost than if a company set up their own in-house HR department, and your staff are already qualified and up to date with all the legal bits of HR.

You only set your HR outsourcing services business up a couple of months ago. You've got a decent website which is easy to get around and contact you through. But your website is new, so you're not ranking very well on search engines for your keywords, and you're not getting much traffic to your website and hardly anyone is enquiring about your services (yet). You want to get more traffic to your website, get some leads, and start getting conversions.

That's where digital PR work comes in.

A great way to get people to your website is to write articles about your business on other websites. You can reach more people by writing on a website that already has good traffic and people reading, show that you're an expert in all things HR so people will trust your services, and include a link to your website so that people can click through and read more about your services.

This is what we call "guest blogging". Guest blogging isn't the same as advertising or writing press releases about your company – instead, you're writing editorial content about your industry that editors see as interesting and valuable without *directly* promoting your business. At the end you can usually include a short author bio about you and a link to your company's website or social media.

But just where do you find publications to pitch your articles to?

1. Hosting your own Content Versus Guest Posting Elsewhere

So you've got a mind blowing content idea wrapped up and spanked on the bottom. Next task is deciding how you will take that content, your message, and deliver it to your target audience. Broadly speaking, you can either a) upload the content to your own website or b) see if another more popular website is interested in running your content for you.

Each option has its own set of advantages and disadvantages. The main advantages of keeping your content on your own website are that it has the potential to drive traffic to your site and can increase the perceived authority of your website. But hosting your own content is a bit of a long game, and unless you have a decent rate of traffic already then there is a real risk that your excellent content will be seen by next to nobody.

Getting your excellent idea onto a different website, perhaps even a national news site, is a surefire way to get a ton of people reading your content and consuming your message. This in itself is excellent for your business. If you can start a discussion online then more people will be talking about your business and more people will be visiting your business. But unlike hosting your own content, it doesn't directly do anything for your own website.

However, if your goal is both to get people talking about your business and also to improve the visibility of your website, *there's a way of doing both at the same time.* The technique is to get your excellent content onto a high profile website, but ensure that your content contains a backlink to your own website along with an author bio that explains who you are and why your business is worth keeping an eye on. This technique enables you to benefit from the high traffic of the website that you posted on, while also diverting a fraction of that traffic to your own website. Some of that traffic will convert; some could even end up becoming repeat customers.

Whether you decide to post on your own website or on someone else's will depend on the goals that you have set for your digital PR campaign, but usually the correct approach is a mix of both. You'll need to do some guest posting to direct some initial traffic to your website, then have some excellent content up there that you can link back to and so that new users have a reason to stay when they arrive!

2. What's Wrong with Duplicate Content?

Now some of you might be wondering "why can't I just upload one copy of the content to my website and another copy of the content to someone else's website?" Good question. When you have one article on one site and a complete copy of that article on another, Google flags that up as duplicate content.

There's no direct penalty for duplicate content (as far as we know, Google is very secretive about its algorithms). Instead, Google simply chooses to show internet users one copy of the article and hide the other copy. Since Google has no way of knowing for sure which of the two (or more) articles is the original, it simply shows internet users the most popular copy and hides the other ones. What this means in practice is that if multiple websites upload a copy of the same article then only one of the websites, the most popular one, gets the SEO benefits.

The other reason that you might want to think about not using duplicate content is exclusivity. By and large, editors from other websites won't be interested in featuring your content unless you give them *exclusivity* and agree not to upload the same content elsewhere.

3. Compiling a List of Target Publications

If you do decide to upload your content elsewhere, the next step is deciding where exactly. There are already well over a billion websites out there, narrowing down this vast number into a list of targets that are well suited to your business and your content is the next task. Lots of our clients come to us and ask if we can get them into *Forbes* or *The Guardian* simply because those are their favourite and the most well-known publications.

But the goal isn't getting into your favourite or even the world's biggest publication – it's getting into your target audience's favourite publication. You may read *Forbes* but are your customers reading it? Look back at the avatar that we developed in chapter two. Ask yourself: where do they get their information? Which publications do they read? If you can answer those two questions, then you have the first names down in your target publication list.

Now we're going to use some tools to check that we have the right demographic. **Quantcast**, a tool that we've mentioned already, provides audience analysis for any website, enabling you to see which demographics are using a particular site.

Google Analytics also gives you extensive demographic data for your website and Google is kind enough to give this valuable information away for free. Through the audience/demographic tab on Google Analytics, you can discover the following information about your website's visitors:

- Language
- Location
- Browser used
- Mobile device used
- Bounce rate
- Average visit duration

Facebook Insights gives you valuable information about what kind of people are visiting your company's Facebook Fan Page. This gives you the following information about the people who like your Facebook page (sex, age, country, city, language). If there's a discrepancy between the people who like your Facebook Page and the people who visit your website, then it's worth thinking about why this might be.

Alexa is an alternative paid for tool for researching a website's demographics. By sending a little bit of money Alexa's way, you get access to a range of

SEO tools, including demographic information about your website's visitors. These stats go right down to their level of education and whether or not they have any children.

Once you have demographic information about your customers, the next step is finding out where your customers hang out online. If you are targeting early twenty-somethings from the United States, you'll have a totally different audience (and therefore will be targeting your PR efforts at totally different locations) than if you are targeting people who are starting a family in the United Kingdom.

4. Adding to your List of Target Publications

Aside from looking at your target audience, there are a number of other ways to identify target publications.

Looking at Key Magazines and Websites for the Industry

If your business is located in a specific niche, then look at the key magazines and websites for your industry. For example, while the mainstream press is (understandably) hesitant to write about a topic like HR in any way shape or form, there are dozens if not hundreds of websites that are completely dedicated to HR and HR alone. If your product or service is especially useful to HR professionals, then getting into one or more of these publications would be a real win for your business.

Looking for Local Magazines and Websites

If you are a business with a physical location, then don't underestimate the importance of local websites and publications. They are much more likely to be used by people who have genuine potential to become customers, and as an additional advantage, local publications are often looking for ways to fill their pages before deadline day. Look for the following:

- Newspapers – local and regional.
- News Websites – often newspapers will have online versions and there may be some online-only news websites or notice boards.
- Local Business Websites – any websites who run articles about or interview local business owners?
- Magazines – any relevant local magazines we could get into?
- Blogs – how about bloggers related to your niche based in Glasgow?

If you're a local business, then a locally based publication with a lower authority will be much more important to your business than a high authority .com website with an international audience. Even though high authority is still better (of course), local is the focus (in this instance).

Googling Keywords, Using " "

Is there a problem that can't be solved by Google? If there is, I don't want to know about it. Simply Google keywords that are relevant to your content and take note of promising looking publications that are ranking well. If you are especially looking for a publication that is open to taking guest posts then you can structure your search something like this: "keywords" + "guest post". You can substitute your keywords and the phrase guest post for similar phrases such as "submit content" or "contribute article" to broaden your search even further.

Identifying Influencers and Where They are Writing

Keep tabs on key influencers for your industry and see where they are writing. The most well-respected websites attract the biggest influencers and vice versa. Simply Google their name to get a comprehensive list of websites where they are mentioned, and scan through them to see the websites where they themselves are authors.

Checking Out a Competitor's Backlink Profile

We've mentioned this tactic before, but using **Open Site Explorer** or **Backlink Watch** to get a list of publications where your competitors have been mentioned is an excellent way of identifying target publications that are likely to be open to hosting your content. Remember that if you only use competitor analysis you will always be behind, but using it as one tool within a larger strategy can help you catch up on competitors that are outranking you.

5. How to Tell a Good Website from a Spammy One

Not all publications are made equal. As Neil Patel, an industry influencer in digital marketing and founder of Quicksprout, warns: "You can Google 'places to guest-blog' and find some spammy sites that will compromise your site, ruin your reputation, and cannibalize your content marketing."

It's vitally important that you don't end up sabotaging your content marketing efforts by uploading your well-crafted content to spammy or disreputable websites. Here are a few ways that you can check if a website is legit:

1. Does it look spammy? Popups, poor formatting, spelling mistakes are all signs of a low quality website.
2. What is the DA? Use your Moz toolbar to check the DA of the website that you are looking at. Anything below 15 is a bit of a red flag unless it's an obviously new and just launched website.
3. What is the spam score? Use **Open Site Explorer** and enter the URL to see a number of metrics, including a spam score, for your target website. You'll get a rating out of 17 that will tell you the likelihood that the website has been penalised by Google

6. Getting into Niche, Industry-Specific and Up-and-Coming Publications

It's almost time for your first pitch! But before we get there, it's important to understand a little more about what the media landscape looks like in 2016.

It's a tough time to be running a small publication or website. Print publications are worried because ad money is moving online. Small online websites are worried because the online world is increasingly competitive, as vast quantities of content are being created everyday. It's getting harder to compete with the larger websites and it's a constant struggle simply to maintain your position in world where everyone is racing forward at top speed. Journalists are being paid less to do more, and lots of writing is being done by unpaid interns or "guest bloggers".

In order to get your content into a small publication, you have to think "what's in it for them?" No one is going to feature your content simply so that you can get free publicity! The most simple thing that you can give an editor is payment. Almost all publications, no matter how prestigious, will feature your article in exchange for a fee. For small publications that fee can be quite reasonable, but of course there are people out there who will ruthlessly overcharge. We'll cover this subject in more detail in our chapter on sponsored content.

The other thing that you have to offer is the content itself. To make it more valuable, it should be exclusive and it should be an exceptionally good idea. Smaller publications may well decide to take your content because they like the idea and they don't have the staff or the time to produce the content themselves. Think about it: if you are doing their job for them (and it's a job they don't quite have time to do), then they will be happy that someone else has stepped in and offered to do it for them!

7. Getting into the National Newspapers

Getting into the national newspapers, or industry leading publications, is more difficult. As before, newspapers will run almost anything that you ask them to for a fee, but that fee is usually beyond what small businesses can afford to pay.

And unlike smaller publications, newspapers still tend to have large teams of skillful journalists (paid or otherwise), so they don't need help creating content. That doesn't mean that you can't get a mention though. While the national newspapers won't simply run a story that you've written, they could well pick up a story that you have created (such as the breast milk ice cream mentioned earlier).

The other route into a national newspaper is through journalists. The key thing to remember about journalists is that they are exceptionally busy. They might have three or four articles that they are writing at any one time and doing the research for all that work is time-consuming. To reduce their workload, journalists often take to channels like **Twitter** or **Response Source** asking for help. They may say something like: "Writing an article on business management, any small business owners have any useful tips?"

Now is your time to strike like a ninja! Be quick, be helpful, and politely remind the journalist to mention your business in the article in exchange for the information. In this way, even the smallest of businesses can be mentioned in the biggest of newspapers. Of course, you have to be hanging out where the journalists are hanging out and have your eye on the ball, but the payoff is truly enormous.

CASE STUDY: GETTING FEATURED IN A NATIONAL NEWSPAPER

One of our clients owned a health-related business and he wanted to get the word out about his service. We followed a number of relevant journalists with a history of health writing on Twitter, and kept our eyes open on Response Source. Sure enough, a few weeks later a request came through: "anyone have any tips for healthy heart week?" We responded right away with an interesting but little-known piece of information, and ended up getting our client, his service, and a link on one of the UK's biggest news websites!

8. Pitching to Editors, Finding Contact Details and Creating a Press List

Getting your story from your head into your target publication is your mission, and there's only one person that stands between you and your objective: the editor.

Editors are gatekeepers; they decide which stories their publication runs and which ones are left out in the cold. They are the person that you are going to have to convince/persuade/bribe if your digital PR campaign is going to be a success. And to make matters more difficult, they receive a metric tonne of story ideas every day, and have a to-do list that stretches off into the horizon. Learning how to communicate with editors is an essential skill that takes some practice to master.

First of all, you're going to have to find the editor of your target publication. The easiest way to do this is through the website. Most websites have a "contact us" page which lists the staff as well as their contact information. Simply create a press list in Excel or Google sheets and note down the name of the editor, their position, the publication that they work for and any contact details that they might have listed (including social media profiles). Job done.

To find the "contact us" tab quickly on a web page, use the search function (ctrl+F on Windows) and search for the phrase "contact" – that should take you straight there. If you still can't find the contact us page, then put the URL in quotation marks in Google then the + symbol then "contact us" also in quotation marks. So finding the contact us page for the UK's #1 small business digital marketing agency would mean typing (including the quotation marks) *"www.exposureninja.com"+"contact+us"* into Google. If that still doesn't work try variations such as "get in touch" or even "meet the team."

Some websites purposefully don't list their staff's email addresses at all. If this is the case, then it could be taken as a good sign – most people probably give up at this point and go somewhere else. But not you. You're going to go the extra mile and send the editor a message on social media. Sending an editor a direct message on Twitter is more likely to get you a response, and because it's under 140 characters it won't take them long to read it. If the staff names aren't listed on the website, simply read through the articles online and check the author byline to see who's working there, then look to connect with these people on social media.

Action Point: Create a press list in Excel or Google sheets. *Get the email addresses and social media information of ten editors whose publications you would like to be featured in.*

9. Writing the Perfect Pitch

Don't send that email just yet!

An editor can easily receive hundreds of emails in a day, so what are you going to do to make yours stand out from the crowd? You're going to have to craft a pitch, and it's going to have to be pitch perfect (sorry).

Crafting a perfect pitch is truly an art form, so take your time while getting started and don't be frustrated if it takes longer than you might imagine to get it right. Before you sit down to write that email or make that phone call, take a moment to consider the situation from the editor's perspective. They're thinking 1) I'm so busy that I don't have time to breathe right now and 2) what's in it for me? Any pitch that you write has to communicate a clear benefit to the editor, and it has to be concise and clear enough to be read, understood, and digested in under two minutes.

Are pitches likely to be more successful if they are made by email or by phone? Increasingly, I'm seeing editors say, "contact me by email only please!" and it's easy to see why. Emails can be dealt with as and when the reader has time to do so and have an additional advantage in that they can contain relevant word or text documents. On the other hand, emails can be ignored more easily and I still talk to the occasional editor if they prefer talking to a person rather than writing to them. I'd say that your default position should be email, but if you consider yourself a better talker than writer, or if there is any indication that the editor prefers a phone call, don't be afraid to give that a go.

Time to get writing. Crafting a strong pitch follows many of the same rules that we discussed in crafting a press release. Your headline needs to be strong enough to elicit curiosity in the very people that spend all day writing headlines. In other words, it needs to be first class. Your subject line should be equally compelling. Remember to tread that fine line between leaving out enough information so that they are curious enough to open the email but including enough information so that they don't dismiss it for being unclear. A brief tag such as (story idea) or (editorial submission) after the subject line is fine for letting the editor know exactly what they are looking at.

Next comes the top line of the email, which should act as a secondary headline to build interest even further. Lastly comes the body itself. Keep it concise (under five hundred words, less is better than more) while also being clear. Communicate key benefits to the editor, such as exclusivity, payment or how you will help promote the story. A last point that you have to hit in a pitch to an editor is "*why you?*" Editors have teams of writers and journalists at their disposal, so if your idea is a good one then what's to stop them researching it themselves and cutting you out of the story? Ways around this are to make your business an integral part of the story so that you cannot be written out of it. Or alternatively, stress your qualifications as a source for their story. Perhaps you are the biggest business within a particular niche or area, or perhaps there is some emotional reason why you are linked to the story?

Lastly, get your email checked by someone who knows their grammar. If there's anyone that's going to judge you on your ability to put together a sentence, it's an editor. They were looking for an excuse to delete your email anyway, a spelling mistake is more than reason enough for them never to get back to you.

Remember too that editors are people, so treat them like people. Anything that has a whiff of "copy+paste" about it will be universally disregarded, but pieces with more personal touches have more pulling power. Mention the editor and publication by name and explain why your story is a good fit for their particular publication in such a way that shows that you are familiar with their work and understand what they are trying to achieve. Flattery can be a useful tactic.

Editors are all different and what works for one may simply infuriate another. There is no magic pitch, only tools that increase your chances of success and reduce your chances of failure. That being said, it is likely that you will at some point in your digital PR campaign come up with a killer idea that is roundly ignored by everyone you send it to. This can be a little heartbreaking, but don't take it personally. So long as you have read and understood the advice in this chapter, it probably doesn't mean that there's anything wrong with your style or your idea – it just wasn't right for these editors at this moment. Put it back in the swipe file, dust yourself off, and start again.

It's hard (but far from impossible) to get a story to stick with an editor. Send out tens if not hundreds of pitches via emails or phonecalls. Be realistic and expect to get a "no" or to get ignored by the majority of them. And then, if this happens, don't panic. Send a polite follow up email to editors that you haven't heard back from. Something along the lines of: "did you get a chance to read my email?" will suffice. You'll be amazed at how many editors genuinely meant to get back to you, but simply forgot due to other pressing concerns.

Here's an example of a pitch from a small business owner who got his 'leggings for men' business into The Daily Express with no connections or budget to speak of:

> "The Daily Express,
>
> You may have seen the recent news articles published by The Telegraph and the Daily Mail (shared 4000 times and received 200 comments) covering the emergence of "Meggings into the Mainstream".
>
> An interesting concept I'm sure you would agree, and definitely a hot topic at the moment. Both of these stories feature a Meggings company from Chicago. We propose that we collaborate on a story featuring an organisation a little closer to home:
>
> sTitch Leggings.
>
> A company founded in 2012 by three London graduates.
>
> *On the 28th of October 2012 two young city workers wore ill-fitting female leggings to a fancy dress party in north London. These two individuals alongside a mutual friend have now tasked themselves with designing, manufacturing and selling male leggings to the fashion-conscious Londoner.*
>
> Let me know if this is of interest to you and we can make the necessary arrangements (we are more than happy to create content if required).
>
> Thank you for your time,
>
> Tom Hunt,
> sTitch Leggings"

This example, featured on HubSpot's blog, did almost everything right and as a result got major coverage for their brand. Let's look at why it succeeded and what we can learn from their success.

A) It piggybacked off a trending topic

Not only did the writer exploit an already trending topic, but they also demonstrated the trend by drawing attention to the 4000 shares and 200 comments.

B) It made life easy for the reporter

The line "more than happy to create content if required" is a killer here. It says to the rushed reporter "I'm happy to do the heavy lifting if you like the story."

C) It appeals to a common bond

The word "London" is mentioned twice in the above article, and with the line "a little closer to home" it becomes clear why: the writer is asking the reporter to help a London-based startup get an edge over a foreign competitor. By suggesting that there are two teams ("us" and "them") and by subtly suggesting that both you and the reporter are part of the "us" camp, you can make it feel like they are doing the *team* a favour rather than just doing you a favour.

> **Action Point:** *Using the advice and example outlined above, write a pitch for one of your story ideas to an editor of your target publication. Get a trustworthy person to read through it, take a deep breath, then press send. Rinse and repeat.*

10. Networking & Follow-up Articles

Success will come at some point, if not in the first month then in the second. Savour it, enjoy it, and do your best to continue to be involved in the story – adding content, replying to comments, or being available for interview if necessary. We're about to get into the actual meat and potatoes of content creation next, but first we're going to briefly emphasise the importance of networking.

Getting your first story is like landing your very first job out of school – it's normal to get a lot of doors in your face before you get your foot in the door. But once you're on the inside things start to get much easier because you have contacts. Once you have contacts in the press, the amount of effort needed to get a story promoted drops dramatically. If you become friends with an editor, they might start coming to you every time they need information on your industry, and you should happily oblige. If you land an article in an industry-specific magazine, don't stop there. If it is successful, ask about writing a follow up article, or even becoming a regular contributor to their website. While the SEO benefits on guest posting do have diminishing returns, the brand awareness benefits can easily accrue over time with a regular slot.

Even editors that turn you down are worth staying in touch with. I had an ongoing dialogue with an editor who shot down five or six of my story ideas, but always took the time to explain why. He was almost as excited as I was when I eventually came up with something that was suitable for his website. Pitching is a hard slog, but persistence does pay. Be tough, be smart, and be hardworking. The harder you work, the luckier you'll get.

Chapter 5

Writing Content, Guest Blogs & Editorials

Well crafted written content can take a casual reader and convert them into a paying customer, or even transform the merely curious into ardent supporters of your brand message. This chapter will teach you how to transform the ideas that you developed in chapter three into content that will make your website rank highly and your business become respected as an authority in your field.

In this chapter:

- Creating a Content Calendar
- Writing for Your Target Audience
- Developing a Brand Voice
- Understanding Tone and its Impact on Your Writing
- How to Actually Write an Article
- Links and Anchor text

1. Creating a Content Calendar

Coming up with excellent ideas is a good start, but simply vomiting those ideas out onto a blog or into a series of articles as and when you feel like it simply isn't the way to go about it. In order for your content to be most effective as a marketing tool, it needs to be part of a planned marketing effort that takes a number of factors into account. In short, you need a *content calendar*.

Picture this: you've worked hard and followed the action points outlined in this book and created a killer first blog post that has heaps of traffic and plenty of engagement. But now your readers are asking "what next?" and you've no idea when the next post will be ready or how it ties in with the last one. You've just missed an excellent opportunity to get your casual readers to turn into repeat readers, and it's all because you didn't create a content calendar to help you plan your writing schedule ahead of time.

A content calendar will enable you to produce content that coincides with key events in the year, such as conferences that are specific to your industry or events that are recognised by the wider public, like holidays, news stories, or the release of the latest blockbuster. Whatever's relevant. It also enables you to visualise the content that you create as a whole so that you can see on a macro level whether any topics have been neglected or need some reinforcing. Using a content calendar will help you patch up any holes that appear in your coverage of your subject with plenty of time to spare.

Lastly, a content calendar is useful because it enables you to stay organised and stick to deadlines. Many blogs or article series start out ambitiously, but trail off once the honeymoon period is over and the duties of the real world rear their ugly heads. It can also help you to think of your blog as an ongoing body of work that is interconnected (and therefore more useful to your readers), rather than a series of separate articles only held together by a common theme. You can even use a content calendar to enable yourself to hit more ambitious goals. Rather than simply aiming to produce twenty random blog posts in a year, you could instead aim to produce twenty blogs that also function as chapters and release the series as a complete book after twelve months.

Creating a content calendar is easy with a free tool such as Google Calendar, and it will mean that you don't miss key events or run out of ideas early and come to a screeching halt. When putting together a content calendar, make sure you do the following:

- Mark out key dates for your industry and tie a blog idea to them. You could write a post on "ten things that we learned from the winter conference" after an important conference, or you might create content targeting a particular group of buyers in the run-up to Christmas.
- Schedule when your content is going to be written, published, and supported by social media activity. Whether you decide to post every

week or every day, it helps to do things on a timetable that your readers can predict.

- Link in your social media activities so that they are running side-by-side with and complementing your PR activities.

Check out this very useful yearly outline from PR goddess Lexi Mills, who has worked as Head of Digital PR for Distilled and on digital PR campaigns for brands including bathrooms.com. Here, she highlights the main digital PR and social media processes. You want your digital PR activities to work side by side with your social media, so plan them alongside one another (see *Figures 1 and 2*).

When you have a basic yearly structure and a digital campaign in place, design a monthly content calendar where you decide on themes for your content. Specify the quantity of content that you plan to produce and then go into detail with what you're going to be writing about and when you're going to be publishing it.

At Exposure Ninja, our Digital PR team uses a colour-coded content calendar. We highlight monthly themes and target keywords, then work our way down researching blog topics and outreach plans based around these.

	January		February		March	
Content Theme						
Target Keywords						
Monthly Events			14th	Valentines		
Blog Topics	1		1		1	
	2		2		2	
Outreach Activities						
Outreach Topics	1		1		1	
	2		2		2	
	3		3		3	
Regular Contributions						

With a content calendar under your belt, it's time to get writing.

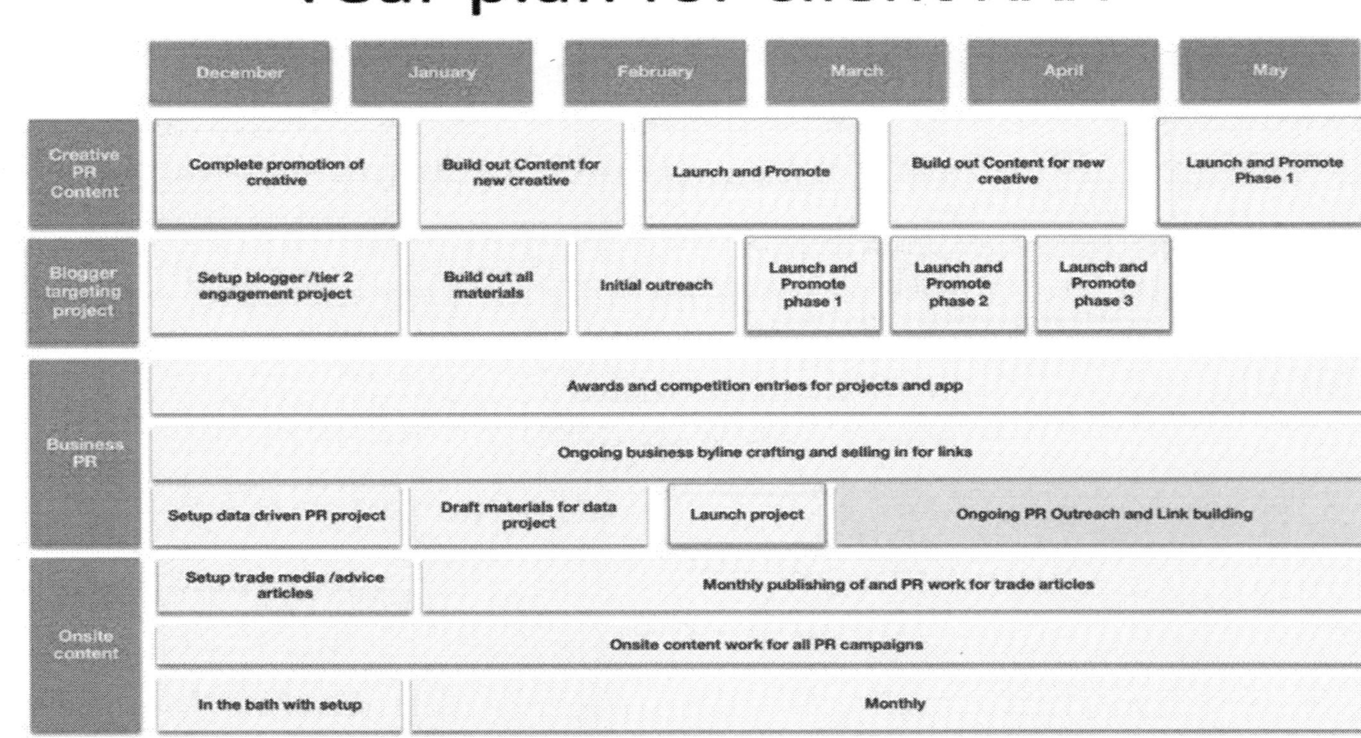
Year plan for client XXX
December
January
February
March
April
May
Creative PR Content
Complete promotion of creative
Build out Content for new creative
Launch and Promote
Build out Content for new creative
Launch and Promote Phase 1
Blogger targeting project
Setup blogger /tier 2 engagement project
Build out all materials
Initial outreach
Launch and Promote phase 1
Launch and Promote phase 2
Launch and Promote phase 3
Business PR
Awards and competition entries for projects and app
Ongoing business byline crafting and selling in for links
Setup data driven PR project
Draft materials for data project
Launch project
Ongoing PR Outreach and Link building
Onsite content
Setup trade media /advice articles
Monthly publishing of and PR work for trade articles
Onsite content work for all PR campaigns
In the bath with setup
Monthly

Figure 1

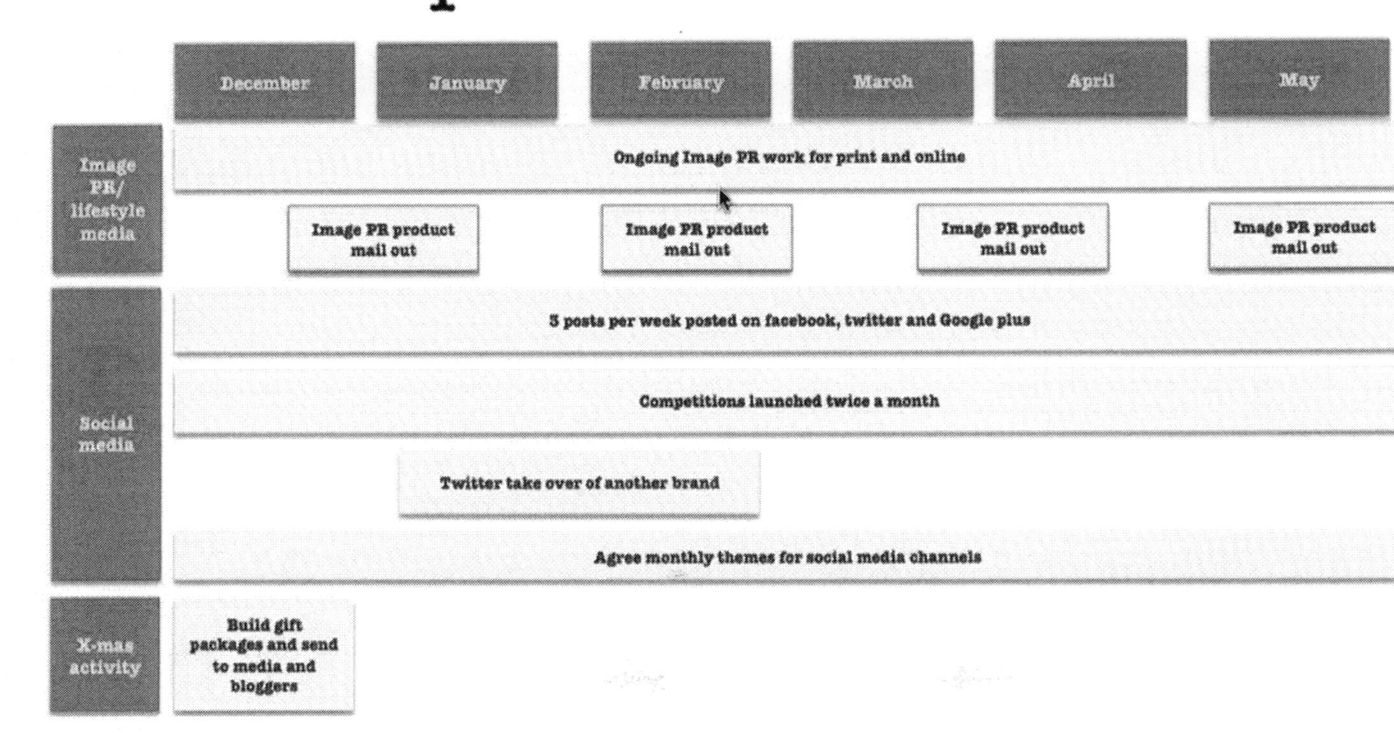
Year plan for client XXX
December
January
February
March
April
May
Image PR/ lifestyle media
Ongoing Image PR work for print and online
Image PR product mail out
Image PR product mail out
Image PR product mail out
Image PR product mail out
Social media
5 posts per week posted on facebook, twitter and Google plus
Competitions launched twice a month
Twitter take over of another brand
Agree monthly themes for social media channels
X-mas activity
Build gift packages and send to media and bloggers

Figure 2

2. Writing for your Target Audience

What's the difference between middlingly successful writing and phenomenally successful writing? It isn't always the quality of the sentence structure or the author's ability to infallibly choose the right word for each moment. In fact, if we look at one of the most successful pieces of writing of the last decade, EL James' bondage-based romp *Fifty Shades of Gray*, we can quickly see that the quality of the writing isn't actually that important at all.

Here's a sample of her writing just for fun: "His voice is warm and husky like dark melted chocolate fudge caramel... or something." But similes like that one didn't stop James from making more money than Croesus.

What's important is that an author understands *who they are writing for* and *what they want to read* and communicates to that audience with language *that they can understand.* EL James may not have won any respect from the critics, but she wrote a piece of fiction that her target audience found deeply satisfying and is rich beyond her wildest dreams as a result of that. There's no such thing as good writing or bad writing – only effective writing and ineffective writing. In this case, your writing is not going to be judged on how many Nobel prizes for literature you receive, but how effective your writing is in helping you to achieve your marketing goals.

If you are not a natural writer or don't consider yourself a particularly literary person, then you should see this as excellent news. It doesn't matter if your writing is a little rough around the edges at places so long as you are writing engaging content that is laser-targeted to your reader. If you are a plumber, write like a plumber. If you are a gardener, write like a gardener. This naturalness will not only make your life simpler, but it will also help you to come across as more authentic to your readers, which is always a winning quality.

To write for your audience, you have to know your audience. Fortunately, we already identified our target audience earlier in the book, so we have a good idea of who they are and what kind of content they like. If you have a number of target audiences, as most businesses do, then consider breaking up your content into different styles that will suit different audiences. If 50% of your customers are demographic A, 30% are demographic B, and 20% of your customers are demographic C, then you could break up your content into similar ratios to appeal to each type of customer. This, of course, is providing that you are never alienating your primary target.

Once you've identified your audience, tailoring your writing to suit your audience is the next step.

3. Developing a Brand Voice

Once you start creating content for your brand, one of the key things that you will need to keep in mind is the brand voice that you are aiming to convey. A brand voice is not what you say — that's the brand message — but how you say it. It refers to your choice of vocabulary, your word order and the length and rhythm of your sentences. Once you've developed a brand voice, you can use it consistently across all of your written content. This includes not only your blogs and articles but also your web copy, emails, and ad campaigns.

Developing a brand voice will help distinguish you from your competitors. Compare:

> **"FOR THAT MOMENT WHEN YOU NEED IT MOST, WHEN THE ENERGY AND THE GOOD TIMES FLOW. WHATEVER YOU DO, DO IT WITH ENERGY."**

with:

> "hello, we're **innocent** and we're here to make it easy for people to do themselves some good (whilst making it taste nice too)"
>
> It will come as no surprise that the first piece of copy was written by an energy drink maker (Lucozade — they have the word energy in there twice!) and that the second piece of copy was written by healthy (but sugar-laden and Coca-Cola owned) smoothie maker Innocent. Both tags play fast and loose with punctuation, but in a way that reinforces their brand message. Lucozade opts for the powerful all caps because they want consumers to associate Lucozade with strength and power. Innocent decide instead to play so innocent that they don't even know how to use punctuation, almost making the copy look child-like.

Compare also the choice of language. Innocent say two things about their product: 1) that it tastes nice and 2) that it does good. Good and nice are two adjectives that you'll be told to steer clear of in any kind of writing class, but that's exactly why they use them. They've chosen simple words because they want to imply that they are a simple product: just juice, no junk.

Lucozade, on the other hand, has gone with the impressively stupid "whatever you do, do it with energy." Want to drive dangerously? Do it with energy. Making a poor life decision? DO IT WITH ENERGY. But it fits entirely with the energy drink philosophy – actions are more important than words (or thinking) – and so ties the brand voice in with the product in a way that is consistent and authentic.

The other key element of a brand voice is that it personifies your business. Brands don't speak; people do. So when your brand starts to speak, the aim is that customers stop thinking of your brand as a faceless entity and start thinking of it as a person. A person that they can trust and feel familiar with. This is why every piece of advice out there on brand voice asks marketers to ask themselves, "if your brand were a celebrity, which one would they be?" Making your brand appear more personable in the eyes of your consumers makes you distinct from your competitors and helps your consumers build a relationship with your brand.

When it comes to creating content for your brand, you should do so with a clear brand voice in mind. To help you identify your brand voice, try asking yourself: why was your company created in the first place? (No, the answer is not "to make shed loads of cash," or at least, that's not the answer as far as your marketing efforts are concerned!) Innocent aim to make drinks that do good and taste nice, so they have a simple voice for a simple aim. Exposure Ninja aims to give small businesses the tools that they need to succeed online, without all the crap, so we go out of our way to understand the needs of small businesses and we write how we speak.

4. Understanding Tone and Its Impact on your Writing

Once you identified the brand voice that you hope to achieve, it's time to tailor the tone of your writing accordingly. Tone might seem a difficult concept to pin down, but it's actually something that we all use all the time in our daily lives. Imagine that you find yourself needing to make a phone call but your mobile is dead. Your best friend is over at your place, so you say:

> *"Hey, dude! Give us your phone, I need to make a call!"*

(You may not talk like this because you may not be a twenty-something American from the nineties, but you get the point). Now imagine the same situation, but you are outside and you are going to have to ask a stranger if you can use their phone call. Let's go one step further and imagine that that stranger is a *police officer*, it's raining, and you feel hungover. Think about the language that you are going to use, and how it is different to the language you would use with your best friend. You might say something like:

> "*Excuse me officer, sorry to bother you, but is there any chance I could borrow your mobile? It's an emergency and mine is broken.*"

Both sentences say more or less the same thing, but the way that message is communicated is totally different. That difference demonstrates what tone is and why it is important. To help you nail tone, we've highlighted a few elements that you can pay particular attention to.

Formal versus informal language. One of the key differences between the way we spoke to that police officer and the way that we spoke to our friend was the formality of the language we used. Formality implies professionalism, respect, and even authority. As a result, formal language works best with professionals, such as medical and legal people, where these attributes are key. On the other hand, formal language can be boring and unpersonable. Informal language is warm and friendly, but it is also associated with being reckless and unprofessional, which might just be fine if you are selling an energy drink. One of the ways that we suggest formality is indirect language. Compare the formal "is there any chance I could borrow your..." to the informal "give me your..."

Yo, dawg! Some red hot slang coming your way! If you have taken the informal route you are probably considering using slang, but it's worth thinking over carefully. Slang is a high risk, high reward activity. If done correctly, it positions your brand as part of the in-group. But if used incorrectly, or in a way that is at odds with your target market, it's at best painfully embarrassing and at worst potentially devastating. The parody Twitter account @BrandsSayingBae calls out the most painful examples of brands Tweeting like a teenager. I defy anyone over the age of 12... actually, anyone with eyes, to sit through all 3:27 of that painful slang-strewn Chevy ad from 2014 on YouTube. Though to be fair, with 900,000 views and counting they must be doing something right.

Technical language, also known as jargon, is hated by many people because it conveys a sense of superiority from the speaker. But that can actually be an advantage should superiority be a selling point of your business – financial services in particular often employ jargon to make themselves appear superior to their customers, and when selling computer hardware objective superiority is an important factor for hardcore geeks. For most businesses most of the time though, the clearer the language the more relatable your brand will be.

Word order and choice of **pronouns** can also subtly affect the tone of your content. Compare "Our product was designed with you in mind" to "You may want this, which is why we do that". First of all, what comes first, your product or your customer? If your customer is the most important part of a sentence, put them first: "*You* may want this, which is why *we* do that." Alternatively, putting the product first and the customer second implies that the product is the more important part of the equation. It's usually not best practice to put your brand ahead of the customer.

5. How to Actually Write an Article

This is it. The moment has come to finally tackle that blank page! The key to writing effectively is to always keep your reader in mind. You are not writing for yourself; you are writing for your potential customers. You have to give you readers something of value. The simplest way to do this is to solve a problem for someone.

Solving a problem is one of the most popular formats for internet writing. When people have a problem these days, one of the first things they do is ask Google for a solution. That's why "how to guides" are so common place.

The key to getting traffic on this kind of article is to be as specific as you can. The more specific the problem and the person you are writing for, the more likely it is that your articles will do well. This is a chance for you to really use your expert knowledge from your business experience to solve a problem that many of your customers have.

What most bloggers do is look on Google to see what everyone else is writing about then try their hand at the same thing. This is actually the complete opposite of what they should be doing. You should be using Google to see which questions haven't yet been answered well, then filling in this "gap in the market" by writing a blog on the subject that is better than everyone else's. Be less "me too" and more "unique selling point."

For example, if I wrote a blog titled "a backpacker's guide to Thailand", there's less than a snowball's chance in hell that I'd rank for that. There are probably tens of thousands of articles like that online already. No matter how good I am as a writer, it's hard to attract an audience when you aren't bringing anything new to the table. On the other hand, the "vegan travel guide to breakfast in Macedonia" is much more likely to rank highly because very few people have written about that topic before. The beauty of the internet is even a niche blog can get tens of thousands of hits because your potential audience is anyone with an internet connection!

The other advantage of writing very specific content is that it can be strongly targeted at your potential customers. If you sell vegan snack bars, then not only will content about vegan snacks rank higher because there's less competition, but it also has a much better chance of converting because the people reading the article are much more likely than the general population to be interested in the product.

6. What is Anchor Text and Why Is It Important?

Anchor Text is the visible, clickable text in a hyperlink. In most internet browsers, it's blue and underlined, like this link to Moz's blog on anchor text.

In the above example, the anchor text is "Moz's blog on anchor text." The link itself points to the webpage "https://moz.com/learn/seo/anchor-text." Anchor text is important because search engines (such as Google) use the anchor text to work out what the webpage that is linked to is about.

So in the example, Google knows that "https://moz.com/learn/seo/anchor-text" is a link to "Moz's blog on anchor text" because **the anchor text tells Google exactly what it is**.

Still with me?

For the same reason, one of the worst examples of anchor text is "click here." When Google reads the anchor text "click here," it learns nothing about the webpage that is being pointed to.

To improve the visibility of your website when you build backlinks to it from your digital PR articles, you want to let Google know *what* is being linked to with the anchor text. Go paintballing in Kilmarnock is an example of strong anchor text because Google reads "go paintballing in Kilmarnock" and knows that the link is probably pointing to a webpage about paintballing in Kilmarnock.

On the other hand, **company names don't make for the best anchor text**. For example, "Happy Smiles" is not great anchor text because Google's robots can't necessarily work out that Happy Smiles is the name of a dental clinic. A better example of anchor text in this example would be something like "cosmetic dentist in Hull".

Now that you get what anchor text is, how it works, and why we use it, let's answer some common questions about using anchor text when building links to your business' website.

How Many Links Should I Include?

So you've got an editor interested in your article topic and you're setting about writing an article with thoughtful research links and links back to your own website (with some good anchor text). Just how many links should you put to your own website in this article though? **One or two is usually enough.**

You don't want to stuff articles with links, especially as that can be irritating to editors and readers. Not to mention that excessive backlinking looks like spam. But then again, if you've got some really relevant blog posts you're linking in, you don't want to miss out valuable info either. Make a firm decision about which links are relevant and which aren't. Then have look at what the editorial guidelines are on the website you're writing for and decide from there.

How Often Should Links be Pointed at my Homepage / Other Webpages?

Though linking to a homepage is okay, you don't want to *just* be linking to your homepage. Hopefully your website has lots of great and informative content – including blog posts (which we discuss later on in the book) – so **you want to have your article links pointing to different pages on your website.**

You always want to make sure you're linking to the most relevant webpage. If you're an e-cigarette business writing about travelling with e-cigarettes, you don't want that article just to link to your homepage. Rather, it could be linked to a useful blog post you wrote on your site about travelling with e-cigs instead. Choose the most relevant webpage to link to, and mix it up in your articles.

Bloggers, writers, journalists, and editors naturally use slightly different phrases (anchor text) when linking to other articles and blogs, and you should to. If you're creating a bunch of articles using the same anchor text again and again and again... well, that doesn't look good. Instead, you should vary the text and use different phrases to describe what a webpage is about. Added to that, you should make sure you're linking to as many different pages on your site as you can.

Where in an Article Should Links Go?

Ideally, you want to embed links **within the body text of the article**. Yes, right in the belly, the same way that you would link to resources, statistics, and quotes you've used from other websites. This allows the links to be a more natural, flowing part of the article rather than just plonked at the beginning or the end of an article. This way, your link becomes another valuable resource you're using to back up what you're saying.

But Hey, Aren't We Just Going to Annoy Editors?

I got it, I read your mind. Getting all those links to your business' website under editorial radar isn't always that easy. Sometimes editors will see links and be up in your grill about how they don't accept links their articles, or they might even start asking for sponsored content fees. Here are some tips for being smooth with your linking (and anchor text) as well as with those editors...

Linking to Blogs Works Well: Informative, awesome, and good looking blog posts are much easier to link to than pages that are advertising your products or services, for example. Create excellent and informative blog content that is worth linking to from articles.

Embed It in the Body Text: Making it natural is another important skill here. Embed links within an article's body text and avoid saying things like "check out my article over here..." and definitely no writing "click here"! Thinking about what anchor text you're using (and being subtle about it!) will definitely help you here.

Remind the Editor that Your Article is Just for Them: Remind the editors that they're getting unique content off of you – and that's valuable for them. This article isn't going to anyone else. It's especially for them. It's written by an expert (that's you) and you're proud to be publishing it with this editor. Yes, flattery helps. Use it sparingly though. Don't be gushing on editors.

Link to Other Stuff in Your Articles: What you don't want is to have written a whole article and to have only thrown one link to your own website's blog post. That totally **sticks out**. Link to other relevant sources, resources, websites and blogs within the article. Editors will often see these as showing the article is well researched, making it more interesting and useful for readers. Don't cram a gazillion links in there though! Around 5 total (including a client link) per 1000 word article should be enough. By the way (again), you don't want to link to any of your competitor's websites!

How about Getting in Difficult Keywords and/or Location Names into Articles?

There's no denying that some target keywords are more difficult to use than others, especially ones with location names attached (e.g. "cosmetic dentist York"). This is where good topic research, publication research, and content planning comes in.

For difficult keywords, look for topics which are as closely related as possible, or for broader topics where you can break it down into specific sections within the article later on. This will make using those keywords much more straightforward and save you from cramming them in where they look funny – which you never want to do.

Researching publications is important here too. You're not going to be getting "cosmetic dentist York" in an article for any old beauty based website. Look for publications that a) deal with dentistry, b) are based in York, or ideally c) are both of those things.

The better fit the publication, the easier naturally getting keywords and links to your website into articles will be.

Chapter 6

Sponsored Content (Why You Shouldn't Believe What You Read in the News...)

Newspapers and news sites have a reputation for being trustworthy sources of information, but marketers can buy a portion of that trustworthiness and use it to achieve their business goals. It's entirely possible to get your business mentioned in practically any publication of your choosing, including prestigious names like *The Guardian, The New York Times* and *Forbes* – even without developing an interesting news story or cultivating your journalistic contacts.

Everything has its price, and a slot in a newspaper or on a website is no different. In this chapter, we will explore sponsored content, when you should consider using it and how even small businesses can use sponsored content effectively.

In this chapter:

- Why Choose Sponsored Content? (and What It Is)
- What Does Successful Sponsored Content Look Like?
- How Much Should You Pay for Sponsored Content?
- Achieving an ROI through Sponsored Content

1. Why Choose Sponsored Content?

Sponsored content is when you pay a publication or website to run your content. It is an example of native advertising because the content you supply is normally designed to look and feel like the content that is on that website already. Readers often don't realise they are reading an ad until they are part way through the article. Sometimes they never realise that what they are reading is paid for.

The supply of content on the internet is enormous right now – an estimated 2.73 million blogs are being written every day. The demand for online content is also enormous, but there are some natural caps and barriers in place. People only want to spend so much of their time consuming content, and it only takes one content creator to make something that can be read by thousands if not tens of thousands of individuals. This means that there is a mismatch between supply and demand, with some websites having a larger supply of content that their current demand.

In this situation it is very difficult to persuade an editor to run your content unless you have a truly exceptional story. In this situation, it may be worth paying the publication a fee to run your content, saving you time and giving you access to a publication of your choosing. If you're thinking: "if I were going to pay money to get my content delivered to my audience, I would purchase banner adverts and be done with it," then you need to read this next part.

Banner advertising and other traditional forms of paid-for media are losing their effectiveness with every passing day. This is because readers are increasingly becoming *banner blind* – they have taught themselves not to look at banners because they know that there is nothing but adverts there. Plenty of eye-tracking data shows that your chances of being looked at in a banner ad are quite literally a lottery. To make matters worse, the continued rise of programs like AdBlock means that a significant chunk of users are simply not seeing adverts at all. Even more worryingly for advertisers, ad blocking is being driven by the young, with 41% of 18–29 year-olds polled admitting to using an ad blocker.

For these reasons and more, sponsored content is becoming an increasingly commonly used tool by advertisers, with advertising spend on sponsored content increasing year on year.

Google, reflecting the view of the the average internet user, is wary of sponsored content. They are concerned about the prospect of companies effectively paying to rank highly for keywords (or at least, they are concerned because in the case of sponsored content, Google itself isn't making any money). They have said that any company or website that runs paid for content could be excluded from Google News completely, though this seems increasingly unlikely as many major news sites blatantly disregard this rule. Google also states that paid for links must be declared and given the nofollow tag. Yet while Google's rules are fairly tight, their enforcement of these rules has been lax... so far. Time will tell whether they will decide to loosen the rules or enforce existing rules more harshly in the future.

Sponsored content has also generated controversy amongst readers and even government regulators who are concerned that sponsored content is misleading the public. It even made an appearance in Season 19 of *South Park*, with "Sponsored Content" being both an episode title and in some senses the main villain of the series. It is important that both publishers and marketers realise that misleading sponsored content erodes the trust between readers and publishers, and that trust is a resource that is quickly spent but very difficult to regain.

2. What Does Successful Sponsored Content Look Like?

Example #1: The Guardian and Roundtable for Sustainable Oil

The Guardian commonly runs sponsored content and has been doing so for many years. As publications go, it is one of the most transparent, featuring a (reasonably) prominent "sponsored by" subheading to avoid deceiving the reader. The below example, sponsored by the *Roundtable for Sustainable Palm Oil*, is a video drawing attention to the need for sustainable palm oil – a concern that ties in with *The Guardian's* environmentalist editorial stance. *The Guardian* clearly distinguishes between sponsored content, supported content, and content that is brought to readers by brands.

Example #2: The New York Times and Shell

The New York Times attracted some controversy when it first began to run sponsored content in 2014 through its T Brand Studio, but they show no signs of relenting after a stint of successful sponsored content campaigns. One of the most interesting decisions that the publication has made in regards

Become a Guardian Member and support independent journalism
George Monbiot

Become a supporter from just £5 per month to ensure quality journalism is available to all. Find out more

Charlie Marchant · subscribe · search · jobs · dating · more · UK edition

theguardian

UK · world · politics · sport · football · opinion · culture · business · lifestyle · fashion · environment · tech · travel · browse all sections

home › environment › wildlife · energy · pollution · climate change

Guardian sustainable business
the palm oil debate

From the Nutella scandal to Indonesia's forest fires: palm oil in 2015 – in pictures

This year exposed palm oil's political, environmental and social ramifications like never before. Here's what happened

Sponsored by:
RSPO

Tess Riley
@tess_riley

Monday 28 December 2015 08.00 GMT

Shares 692 · Comments 13

Save for later

Wilmar commits to zero deforestation

At the start of this year the world's largest palm oil trader, Wilmar, committed to zero deforestation. However, since the company buys around one third of its raw supply from franchised or independent smallholder farmers who have little regulatory oversight, sceptics are not convinced that Wilmar will be able to stick to its promises.
Photograph: Hotli Simanjuntak/EPA

Palm oil expansion continues in West Africa

Burgeoning global demand for palm oil and increasingly limited space for industry expansion in Asia is leading companies to look increasingly to Africa. Emmanuel Ngalle, pictured here with his grandchildren, refuses to sell his few hectares of land to Socapalm, a private oil palm company

Example #1: *The Guardian and Roundtable for Sustainable Palm Oil*

Example #2: *The New York Times and Shell*

to sponsored content is use of the "paidpost.nytimes.com" URL, making it easy for readers to see sponsored content.

Example #3: *The Economist* and Microsoft

The Economist have taken an unusual format with their sponsored content by holding sponsored debates. In the above example, "Should companies do most of their computing in the cloud?" the debate is sponsored by Microsoft (and indicated as such via the box in the top-right corner of the screen). The "yes" and "no" positions are represented by experts in the field. During the debate, readers can send their questions to a moderator for consideration. Readers vote on who they think they makes the best case and may change their vote at any point during the debate. Voting results and statistics are made clearly available to the readers (in this case, 64% of people agreed that companies should do most of their computing in the cloud).

Example #4 *BuzzFeed* and Android UK

Perhaps no website does sponsored content better than *BuzzFeed*, a website that was built purely as a sponsored content machine. The above example, ruthlessly promoted multiple times on the *BuzzFeed* main page, is just one reason why *BuzzFeed* makes $100 million each year (compare that to the $30 million that *The Huffington Post* was making when it was bought by AOL). It's a simple formula – pick a clickbait-y headline that resonates with the reader, make use of the easily digestible list formula, and totally boss social media – but it's one that has quietly see the company become perhaps the most innovative media corporation of the last decade.

Now it's unlikely that any small or medium-sized business owners will be on any of the above websites as sponsored content (we're about to tackle pricing in the next section) but we can learn a couple of things from their approach.

1. Sponsored content should appear native. It's important that the reader feels that your content is a natural part of their reading experience and doesn't feel disjointed when they come across your message. Looking at the above examples, we can see how each brand has tailored their content format to suit the publication. A formal debate is something we expect to see in *The Economist* whereas listicles (list-based articles) are what *BuzzFeed* is made of.

Cloud computing

Should companies do most of their computing in the cloud?

May 26th 2015 to Jun 5th 2015

Debate Complete

ENTER THIS DEBATE ▸

Sponsored by Microsoft

MICROSOFT'S PERSPECTIVE ▸

ABOUT SPONSORSHIP ▸

REPRESENTING THE SIDES

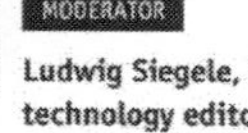

MODERATOR

Ludwig Siegele, The Economist's technology editor

Ludwig Siegele is *The Economist*'s technology editor. He joined the newspaper as US technology correspondent in 1998. In 2003 he went to Berlin as Germany correspondent, relocated to London in 2008 to cover the IT industry until 2011, and then ran part of *The Economist*'s website as online business and finance editor. He started his journalistic career in 1990 as the Paris business correspondent of *Die Zeit*, a Germany weekly. In 1995 he moved from France to California to write about the internet for several German publications. He is co-author of a book on SAP, "Matrix der Welt: SAP und der neue globale Kapitalismus" and is the author of *The Economist's* special report on startups.

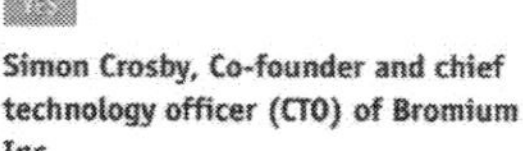

YES

Simon Crosby, Co-founder and chief technology officer (CTO) of Bromium Inc.

Simon Crosby is a co-founder and chief technology officer (CTO) of Bromium Inc., a pioneer of micro-virtualisation, which enables PCs to defend themselves by design from all malware. Previously he was CTO, data centre and cloud, at Citrix Systems, which acquired XenSource, where he was co-founder and CTO; a principal engineer at Intel, where he led strategic research on platform security and trust; and founder and CTO of CPlane Inc., a pioneer in software defined networking. He was a faculty member in the computer laboratory at the University of Cambridge from 1994 to 2000.

NO

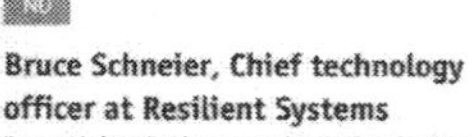

Bruce Schneier, Chief technology officer at Resilient Systems

Bruce Schneier is a security technologist. He is chief technology officer at Resilient Systems, a cyber-security firm, a fellow at Harvard University's Berkman Center and a board member of the Electronic Frontier Foundation (EFF). His latest book is "Data and Goliath: The Hidden Battles to Collect Your Data and Control Your World". He blogs and tweets at @schneierblog.

View all archived >

Example #3: *The Economist* and Microsoft

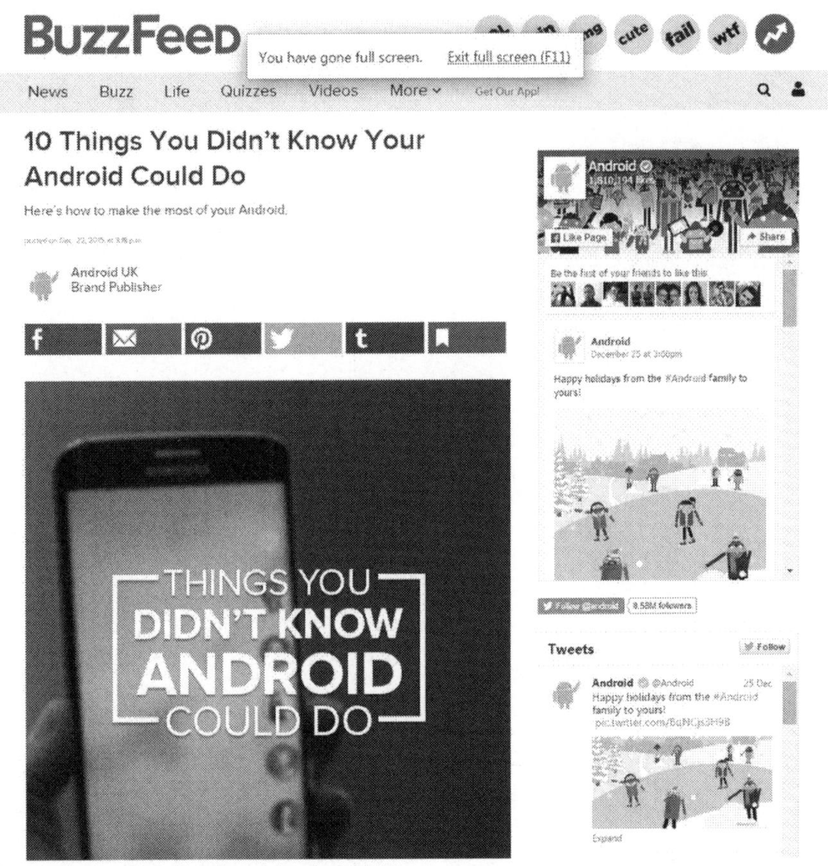

Example #4 *BuzzFeed* and Android UK

2. Yet you shouldn't *get caught* deceiving readers. Each of the above four publications marked the sponsored content as such so that their readers didn't feel cheated or lied to. This is good practice, as readers hate to be taken for fools and won't think highly of brands that treat them as such.
3. Sponsored content does not mean substandard content (if anything the opposite should be true). In the early days of advertorials, brands didn't pay that much attention to the quality of their sponsored content. It was enough to be in the publication, and the quality of the content was an afterthought. Now that advertorials are near-universally hated for their poor quality, they've realised that this was a colossal mistake. Brands *do* have access to some pretty cool resources, such as an advertising budget and industry insights. When they use them

to create sponsored content of a high standard that perhaps even a professional journalist might have struggled with, the sponsored content will get most attention and be most effective as a marketing tool. In other words, now that you've paid for the soapbox you better be sure that you have something interesting to say!

According to a BIA/Kelsey study, not only is everyone doing sponsored content but everyone is also doing pretty well out of it. Consumers are 25% more likely to read a native ad than they are to read a banner ad, and experience an 18% bump in purchasing intent. Different studies show different results, but overwhelmingly agree that native ads are more effective than banner ads and translate to higher commercial intent.

3. How Much Should you Pay for Sponsored Content?

Sponsored content has become the name of the game for publishers, with an estimated 78% of publishers admitting to running sponsored content. Only 10% of publishers flat-out refuse to run sponsored content on their website in the name of journalistic integrity. This means that there's lots of advertising money sloshing around the internet at the moment. How much of yours should you be spending on sponsored content? This subsection will reveal what companies are paying and how you can negotiate the best price for getting your brand name heard.

As of 2016, clear industry-standard pricing plans for sponsored content have yet to be developed. In fact, aside from the reach and influence of the target publication, the single thing that will most likely determine how much you pay is your ability to negotiate a good deal. One of the largest studies to date on sponsored content comes from Chad Pollitt, who conducted a survey of 550 publications to determine the average price that a publication will sell a spot on their website for. They identified the following 17 metrics used to establish pricing:

1. Word count
2. User time on page (based on determining the amount of time a typical user spends on their page)
3. Links, including important details such as number, location, and whether or not they would be "nofollow" links

4. Lead capture, publishers with strong analytic software could charge on a per-lead basis
5. Impressions (CPM): cost per thousand impressions (an impression is the display of an ad while a user is on the page)
6. Amount of work needed to be done by the publication's editorial team
7. Monthly website traffic
8. PageRank
9. Domain Authority
10. Page-level engagement (measuring how much an article is read and engaged with)
11. Social media promotion
12. Email promotion
13. Display advertising (combining sponsored content with traditional banner ads)
14. Number of articles
15. Visibility time
16. Verticals: for large publications that cover many verticals or subject areas
17. Pay-per-click (measure by number of users that click through to the landing page)

Being a number-junkie, Chad then crunched the data to come up with the following terrifying but accurate (or should that be terrifyingly accurate?) formulas:

- Blog Price Formula = -60.5 + 5.97(DA) + 0.978(thousand Fb fans) + 15.1(PR) - 0.000007(AR)
- Publication Price Formula = -37000 + 314(DA) + 20.9(thousand Fb fans) + 5152(PR) – 46.6 (thousand Pinterest followers)

DA stands for Domain Authority, Fb stands for Facebook, PR stands for PageRank and AR stands for AlexaRank. PageRank is a score devised by Google to measure a website's relevance, while AlexaRank is a similar tool developed by alexa.com. What all these numbers boil down to is that the average price of getting sponsored content onto a blog is £196.88, while the average price of getting content into a publication is £4,215.69. Bear in mind that these numbers are averages, based on self-reported data, and come from early 2015 – not very long ago in real terms, but a distant memory for a new trend like sponsored content.

While you may use this formula to help you determine a fair price for a position on smaller blogs and publications, you'll find that all the larger publications and many ambitious smaller ones already have a pricing plan that they are happy to discuss with you. For instance, getting a spot on *Forbes* costs $50,000 per month for a minimum of three months, but you can write as many articles as you like during that time. *Business Insider*, on the other hand, will allow you to upload an article for as little as $5,000 a pop.

4. Achieving an ROI through Sponsored Content

Before you hand over any of your hard-earned money to a publisher, you should negotiate to be sure that you are getting the fairest possible price and that both parties are clear on exactly what the agreement means. Make sure to cover key details such as links (nofollow or otherwise) and visibility time. Most publications and bloggers will have either a media kit or a media package containing key metrics that will help you decide whether the investment is likely to be a good one. You can use this, alongside your own research, to determine how many readers you are likely to get, what the engagement levels might be, and then you can start to estimate roughly how many leads your content will generate. Once you have that estimate, you can start to negotiate what both parties consider to be a fair price.

To keep the price down, there are a few things that you can do:

1. Reduce the work needed to be done by the editorial team and the blogger to the absolute minimum, including doing tasks such as sourcing images and proofreading for grammar errors. The less time that the blogger or publication have invested themselves, the less they are likely to charge for the service.
2. Attempt to secure a deal on a per-lead basis. Most publications and bloggers will be reluctant to do this – they want to be paid regardless of whether or not your content is successful. But it can strongly be argued that the value of the content is directly linked to the amount of leads that it generates. The higher your lead-conversion rate, the better a deal like this could be for your business.
3. Consider asking for a discount on repeat purchases. There are diminishing returns on investment for each article in terms of strict SEO benefits, so you should be able to argue that second and third purchases be discounted.

There are also a couple of red flags to watch out for:

1. Limited visibility time. Often publications will feature sponsored content for a limited time only, to prevent their website from appearing overly spammy. Of course, in most cases you want your article to remain live indefinitely. In some exceptional cases, on some exceptionally popular websites, it may be acceptable to agree to limited visibility time. Though you'll need to work out whether this is worthwhile on a case-by-case basis.
2. How the sponsored content will be presented. Will it be clearly marked as sponsored content, and if so, how so? It *generally* pays to play by Google's rules, so sponsored content that is marked as such isn't necessarily a bad idea. But it should still be formatted and packaged in a way that is attractive to readers.

Once you have a price agreed, determining your ROI is a simply a matter of comparing the cost of the sponsored content to the number of leads that it generated. You can use Google Analytics to see how many of your website visitors are coming through a particular link, then use your lead-conversion rate to calculate roughly how many of those visitors went on to become customers. In addition, some of your content's readers may not have necessarily followed the link but instead came through as organic traffic later on. If there is a spike in your web traffic after your sponsored content is published, estimate what percentage of that is due to the post and add that to your ROI score for the content.

After you have compared your ROI to the amount of time and money spent on creating and securing the content, it's time to analyse it in terms of your overall goals for your digital PR campaign. If it was a success, great! What can you do next time to make it even more successful? If it was a failure, why exactly was it a failure? If the content got less readers than a typical post on that website, perhaps you need to reevaluate your content creation process. If you didn't secure as many leads as you hoped you would, perhaps you should work on your website's conversion rate before restarting your efforts at sponsored content.

Remember too that, as always, targeting the right publication for your target audience is just as important with sponsored content as it is with any other type of content marketing. If your typical customer is a 35-45 year-old Welsh woman with a love of gardening, then your sponsored content needs to be in a publication that is widely read by that demographic.

Chapter 7

Introducing Bloggers & Influencers: Who They Are and Why Your Business Needs Them

Influencers are early-adopters who have used blogging, vlogging (video blogging), and social media to make a name for themselves, establish a personal brand and become an influencer in their niche. A whopping 81% of the population trusts the advice they get from bloggers, making them very powerful advocates for any brand online.

In this chapter:

- 5 Ways Businesses Can Work with Bloggers
- Identifying Bloggers Relevant to Your Business
- What Working with A-Listers Really Means
- Ultimate Tips & Tools for Finding Bloggers in Your Niche
- How to Measure Blogger Influence

Influencer marketing is poised to be "the next big thing" according to Adweek. According to Google Trends, the phrase is a "breakout" – something that is achieving greater than 5000% growth. But what is influencer marketing and how can we use it to build our brand and sell more of our products?

Influencer marketing is the practice of encouraging influential people to recommend your product or service to the people that they have influence over. It essentially borrows and builds on time-worn marketing concepts such as marketing induced word of mouth recommendations and celebrity endorsements. Where influencer marketing differentiates itself from its predecessors is that it generally refers to online influencers who make their influence felt through their blog posts and social media updates.

The arrival of social media means that influencers have more influence than ever before. Literally hundreds of thousands, if not millions, of people see every single Tweet made by celebrity superstars such as Kim Kardashian. If she recommends a product via Tweet, the commercial landscape for that product shifts dramatically and immediately. Influencers aren't new – Edward Bernays, the grandfather of PR, wrote about the importance of what he called "special pleaders" as early as 1927. But what is new is the sheer quantity of people that influencers have access to and communicate with on a daily basis. If Bernays' special pleaders were important, then today's superstar Twitter and YouTube influencers are an order of magnitude more important.

In one exceptional example of how to do influencer marketing properly, Lord & Taylor identified fifty Instagram fashion influencers and asked them to wear the same dress on the same day. The results were as impressive as you might imagine. When impressionable Instagramers saw that all the cool kids were wearing the same dress, they rushed out to the shop to buy one for themselves. The dress sold out the next weekend.

This case study confirms what both theory and research have long been suggesting. A study from McKinsey found that marketing-induced consumer-to-consumer word of mouth generates more than twice the sales of paid advertising as well as an improved retention rate.

The excellent thing about influencer marketing, from a small business point of view, is that it is so new that only a small number of people are doing it properly. This means that influencers (aside from the obvious megastars) aren't yet aware of the true value that they can bring to your brand. In other words, you can currently make use of influencers for a smaller price that they should be charging – but that won't last for much longer. Getting Kim Kardashian to take part in your marketing campaign might be a tall order, but making use of up-and-coming or niche influencers on underexploited platforms like SnapChat and Periscope is a way to make big profits. Much like how it was once possible with Facebook advertising in the early days before everyone else cottoned on.

Unlike traditional editors, bloggers and influencers won't just accept content from business owners simply because they are an industry expert. Working with bloggers is a whole different ball game to working with editors. While editors are after article contributions and expert insight to fill their pages, bloggers are used to running the show by themselves and aren't usually in desperate need for extra content. The vast majority of bloggers write their own content and they put a lot of effort and passion into their craft – which is why they end up with so many adoring readers. Bloggers aren't going to let just anyone publish on their website, which they are often fiercely protective of, especially not anyone who has an alternate agenda.

5 Ways Businesses Can Work with Bloggers

Enticing an influencer to work with your business means giving them a little something extra, especially if you want to slap a link back to your website (which you do) in there. There are a number of different options when it comes to working with bloggers and which one you choose will depend on your business and your digital PR strategy. Here are five of the most successful ways that you could collaborate with bloggers to promote your business:

1. Sponsored Posts

Sponsored posts are when a blogger is paid to write and publish a blog post in their own style which mentions and includes a link to the brand. Sponsored content comes in a variety of forms, some more overt than others – which is often at the blogger's discretion. The Advertising Standards Authority (ASA) regulations state that a blogger should include a disclaimer that the post was sponsored by the brand and there will usually be a short line at the end of the blog post stating this.

Approach bloggers with an idea of a sponsored post topic that is relevant to your brand and their blogging niche. For a travel company this could be something as simple as "10 essentials to pack for your summer holiday." Offer bloggers a token amount of between £25-150 to write a blog post related to this topic that includes a link to a blog post on your own website. In this case, that blog post could be "5 secrets to more efficient holiday packing."

2. Product Reviews

A popular strategy for many businesses is to send products to an influencer in exchange for a review on their blog, a video about their experience, or to share x number of photos on social media. A business could send a blogger an item of clothing, invite them for a complimentary hotel stay, offer them a free beauty treatment, or any number of things. If a influencer loves the product, they will definitely say so in their review – which means that finding influencers who are a good match for your brand and products is vital.

3. Product Features

Product features work the same way as reviews. However, instead of a formal review, a blogger will include the product/service in a blog post about a broader topic relevant to the blogger's niche or as part of a collection of products. For example, a travel blogger might write about the epic mountain that they just climbed and casually mention that they were wearing your trainers while they did it. Feature types vary between genres and between individual bloggers – features include formats such as gift guides, makeup tutorials, recipe posts, fashion lookbooks, and so on.

4. Giveaways

Want to massively boost social media followers or gain subscribers to your newsletter as a way to bring in new customers? Running a giveaway is the answer. For giveaways, the business provides the prize and the influencer will host the competition on their blog post, YouTube channel, or other social media platform. In some cases, the brand may also provide the blogger with a product, or pay the blogger for hosting the giveaway, depending on the authority of the blogger and style of content required.

5. Blogger Events

If you want to gain lots of coverage from bloggers all in one go, then hosting a blogger event is the way to go! Blogger events are put on with the sole purpose of gaining coverage on blogs and getting bloggers excited about your brand. They work particularly well for big brands and for local businesses based in areas where there is a high density of relevant bloggers (e.g. London, Bristol, Brighton). Bloggers are invited to attend an event showcasing your brand in exchange for blogging about it.

Identifying Bloggers Relevant to Your Business

Influencers who are producing content within a specific niche will often have very targeted audience – if your brand aligns well with theirs, then you have a good chance of getting your products or services promoted and therefore getting access to very relevant readers and potential new customers. Remember that having a mismatched blogger/brand relationship is awkward for both the blogger (who risks losing the respect and trust of their readers) and the brand (who won't see much of a return on their investment with a disengaged blog audience).

Just because an influencer has an authoritative website or a big social media following, that doesn't mean you should necessarily work with them. You want to identify which influencer niche is most relevant to your business and partner with influencers within that niche in order to establish a working relationship that's awesome. This will also ensure that your business is getting in front of the right readers. There are a number of factors that you need to consider before you start looking around for influencers to collaborate with:

Target audience	Consider demographics, such as age, gender.
Product Type	Would this influencer and their rea ders/followers/subscribers be interested in your product? Does their blog feature other products of this type?
Product Specifics / Style	Does the influencer's branding, content, and personal style reflect a similar style to your own brand? Does your product fit in well on this blog? Do you like the content of this blog?
Cost of Products	Are your products within the reader's price range? Look at the cost price of other products featured by the influencer and work from there.
Location	Are you a location based business or do you also sell products online? What countries do you ship products to? Where do you get the most orders from? Consider bloggers based in these areas.

Let's say we're a shop selling retro and vintage women's clothing, all with mid-range price tags. They have a small independent shop which is based in Brighton, but they've also started selling their clothes online through their own website. They want to work with bloggers so that they can build their own website's authority through reviews and gain a little social media coverage too. There are a couple of things to unpack about the kind of bloggers who this retro and vintage clothes brand would want to work with (refer to the table on the next page):

Once you have all of the key information, you can decide what kind of bloggers are most relevant to your business. Carrying on with our vintage clothes shop, it's clear that fashion and personal style bloggers will be their main target. They would be looking for personal style bloggers who would model their clothes in lookbooks or vintage clothing blog posts. The business may also decide to branch out and target lifestyle bloggers and beauty bloggers who have a retro/vintage style.

Target audience	*The target audience for the clothing are women, which means the brand will be looking to work with female bloggers (or male bloggers writing for women).*
Product Type	*The business only sells clothes and accessories, so they need bloggers who are interested in clothing, fashion and style.*
Product Specifics / Style	*The brand has a specific retro and vintage style, so they are looking for bloggers who have an affinity with this style.*
Cost of Products	*Readers won't want to see cheap handbags on a high-end fashion blog and equally readers with a tight budget won't want to see products too far above their price range.*
Location	*Let's say our vintage clothes shop is based in Brighton, though they also have an online store. The main focus will be on the UK and preferably Brighton-based bloggers, but if they ship overseas it could be worth considering bloggers based abroad.*

Working with Bloggers in Multiple Niches

Depending on the products and/or services that your business provides, there may be more than one relevant type of blogger to work with. For example, if your online store sells sportswear then your products may be relevant to fitness bloggers, yoga bloggers, fashion bloggers and even active/adventure travel bloggers. Some blogger niches are more receptive to working with brands than others. As you start to get in touch with bloggers about possible working relationships, you will be able to see which bloggers are the most digital PR-friendly and interested in your specific products or services.

What Working with A-Listers Really Means

When you initially start searching for influencers to work with, it's likely that you'll come across a lot of the influencer A-listers. A-list influencers are what we would call the elite in influencer circles, and are comparable to trying to work with Forbes, Huffington Post and other high-end publications that we've all heard of for editorial. Everybody wants to have their company on the front of TIME Magazine. Likewise, everyone wants to be featured on the homepage of the biggest blogger in their industry.

As you can probably guess, the demand for getting content in those places is high – and so is the price tag. While it would be totally rocking to have these influencers promoting your brand and you should definitely aim high, top bloggers and vloggers like Zoella, Lily Pebbles and JJ Olajide (aka KSI) charge up to £4,000 per mention of a product and the same again per Instagram/Twitter post featuring a product. That's a whole lotta dolla for a Tweet!

But there are plenty of awesome bloggers out there who have super engaged audiences and don't charge sky-high prices for a product mention and some Tweets. Most bloggers fall into the mid-level influencer category, where they are still producing great content and have an engaged audience but haven't crossed over into the world of insane stardom where their demands go through the roof. What you want to do is find that blogger sweet spot (unless you have Coca-Cola's advertising budget, in which case you can afford to be indiscriminate!)

How to Find Influencers in Your Niche: Ultimate Tips & Tools

You've got an idea of the kind of influencers you want to work with and some thoughts on what you might offer them, but *how do you find them?* There are a number of different methods that you can use to find influencers in your niche and usually a combination of these different approaches is best to dig up a strong cross-section of relevant influencers.

As you start searching, you want to make a list of all of the influencers whose content is good and who fit well with your brand. Creating a simple Excel spreadsheet with a column for blog URL, the name of blogger, and (if relevant) the blog niche will be all you need. You can then look up their stats later on to make sure they reach far enough and could actually benefit your brand.

Important note: as you research influencers you will notice that some bloggers own their own domain names (normally .com or .co.uk) and some of them are free subdomains (.blogspot.com or .wordpress.com). So the guys at electrictobacconist.com have their own domain while Dick from dickpuddlecotes.blogspot.com has a subdomain which is being hosted by Blogger (previously known as Blogspot). If your primary goal of working with bloggers is SEO then you want to exclusively work with bloggers that own their own domain. This is because links from free subdomains are worth much less than links from actual domains. However, if your primary goal is brand awareness, then you shouldn't necessarily write off free subdomains as some of these blogs still have great engagement with their readers.

Using Google Searches to Find Bloggers

Google Search: Google is a good place to start your blogger search. Search for a simple blog type term, such as "fashion bloggers UK" or "vintage fashion blogs UK" to pull some relevant results. You're likely to find that most of the first page of the search will give you lists of top bloggers published by other websites, as well as the most high profile bloggers for that niche.

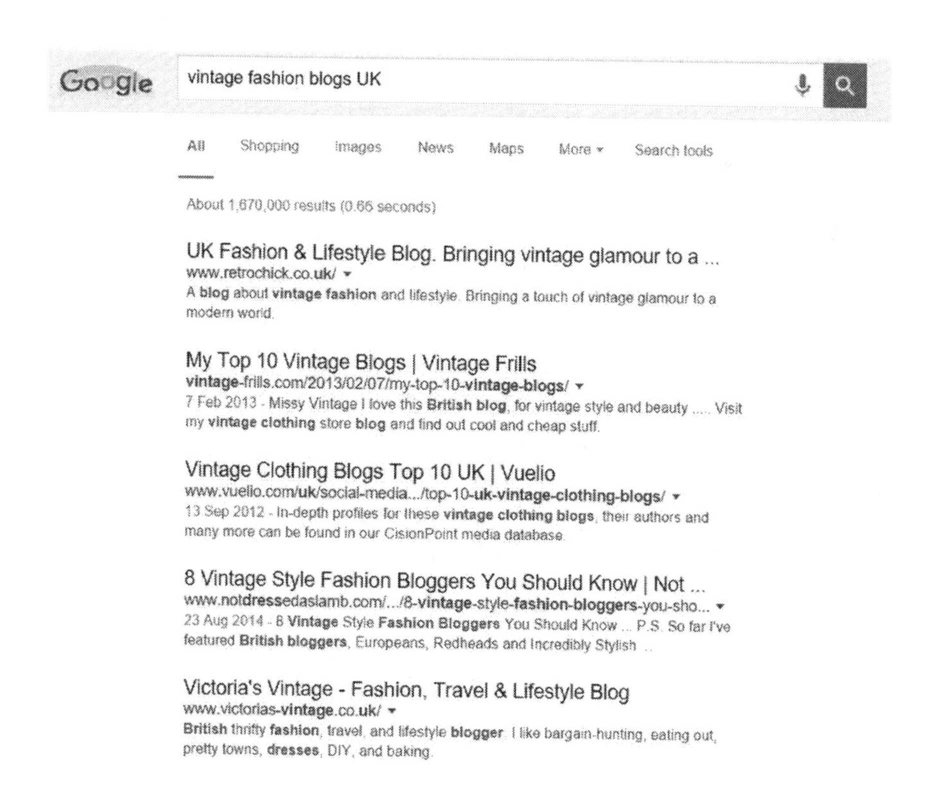

That's exactly what happens if we Google "vintage fashion blogs UK". The second and third results are for top 10 lists featuring multiple bloggers – these are definitely worth checking out, though after you've read a few they will likely become very samey. **Vuelio** is a common top result for lists of influential bloggers. The first, fourth and fifth results on this page are vintage fashion bloggers – retrochick.co.uk, victorias-vintage.co.uk, and notdressedaslamb.com. You can check out these bloggers and see if they look relevant to your brand.

Google Alerts: Set up Google Alerts for the keywords that describe your target angle or blogger. For example, you might want to monitor the word "lipsticks" so that you know whenever a blogger posts an article about lipsticks and potentially reach out to them with your own product to review. You might monitor a generic term such as "gifts for children" if you have products that would be relevant for blog posts that would turn up on parenting, family and mummy blogs.

Blogrolls: Blogrolls are lists of blogs compiled by a blogger in the same niche. You can search on Google for "blogroll" and "specific keyword" to find some relevant blogrolls. For example, if we search "blogroll" + "vegan food" we get a whole list of bloggers with lists of vegan food related blogs.

VEGETARIAN/PESCETARIAN FOOD BLOGS

THE CURVY CARROT

A mostly vegetarian (occasionally pescetarian) blog by a medical student/home cook. I like her because she's unpretentious, smart, and her recipes are always spot on.

VEGAN FOOD BLOGS

FAT FREE VEGAN

Susan's was one of my go-to blogs when I started learning to cook. Accessible, simple, healthy and delicious.

OLIVES FOR DINNER

The vegan blog that taught me how to make vegan mozzarella. Always coming up with food science-y concoctions that I could never dream of thinking up, and her food always looks perfect enough to be plated up at the fanciest of restaurants.

POST PUNK KITCHEN

Isa is a pioneer in vegan cooking. 'Nuff said.

BLOG ROLL

JANUARY 1, 2012 BY RICHA – 2 COMMENTS

Some of my favorite blogs…

VEGAN

An Unrefined Vegan http://anunrefinedvegan.com/
AstigVegan http://astigvegan.com/
Bittersweet http://bittersweetblog.wordpress.com/
Cupcakes and Kale http://cupcakesandkale.blogspot.com/
Chocolate Covered Katie http://chocolatecoveredkatie.com/
Choosing Raw http://choosingraw.com/
Diet Dessert and Dogs http://www.dietdessertndogs.com/
Fat Free Vegan Kitchen http://blog.fatfreevegan.com/
Happy go Lucky Vegan http://happygoluckyvegan.blogspot.com/
Have Cake Will Travel http://havecakewilltravel.com/
Healthy Happy Life http://kblog.lunchboxbunch.com/
Keepin It Kind http://keepinitkind.com/
Namely Marly http://www.namelymarly.com/
Oh She Glows http://ohsheglows.com/
Olives for Dinner http://www.olivesfordinner.com/

Using Twitter to Find Influencers

99.9% influencers use Twitter. If they're Tweeting regularly and using hashtags relevant to their niche, then you'll soon be able to find some of the most active influencers out there by searching directly on Twitter.

Search Hashtags: By searching relevant hashtags, you'll be able to find bloggers and other influencers who have recently Tweeted their content. Here are some of the most common hashtags used in common blogger circle

Beauty bloggers	#bbloggers (beauty bloggers) #motd (makeup of the day) #hotd (hair of the day)
Fashion bloggers	#fbloggers (fashion bloggers) #OOTD (outfit of the day) #WIWT (what I wore today)
Lifestyle bloggers	#lbloggers (lifestyle bloggers)
Home bloggers	#home #interiors
Food bloggers	#foodie #sogood
Fitness bloggers	#fitness #workout #gym
Mummy bloggers	#mummybloggers #pbloggers (parent bloggers)
Travel bloggers	#ttot (travel talk on Twitter) #travel
Tech bloggers	#tech #techblogger

If you are looking to work specifically with bloggers based in a certain area, check to see if there is a hashtag for bloggers located there. For example, bloggers in Brighton use #BrightonBloggers, bloggers from Leeds use #LeedsBloggers, and in Bristol some local bloggers run @BlogClubBristol where members use the #BlogClub hashtag.

Check Out #PRrequest: The #PRrequest hashtag is used by bloggers looking for opportunities to work with brands and by businesses looking for opportunities to work with relevant bloggers. The #journourequest and #bloggerswanted hashtags are useful for getting in touch with journalists and bloggers respectively.

Search Twitter Bios: When you type a keyword into the search bar on Twitter, you can click on the "Accounts" tab so that the search results only show users with those keywords in their Twitter bio. If we search for "lifestyle blogger" and go on the accounts tab, this will pull up all accounts with those words in the profile – that's a whole lot of lifestyle bloggers!

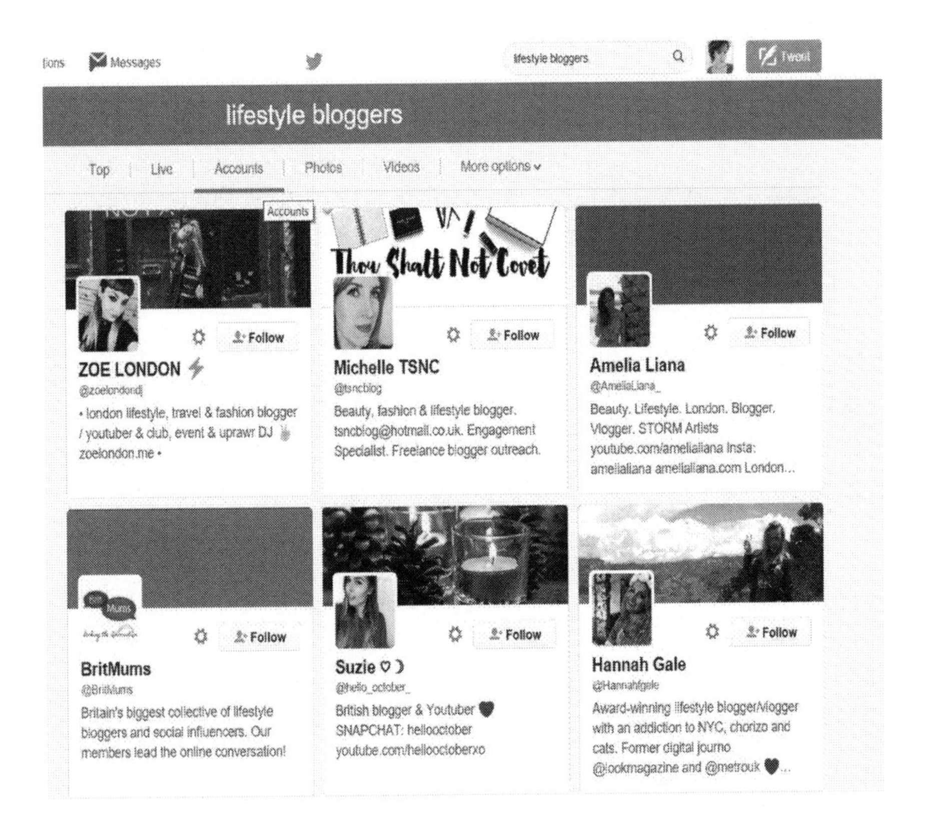

Have a Look at Some Twitter Chats: Twitter chats are live Twitter events about a particular topic. These chats use a specific hashtag to filter all of the Tweets into a single stream of conversation. Twitter chats are usually industry specific and run at a set time every week.

There are Twitter chats for nearly everything, from common blogging chats like #BlogHour and #blogtacular, to ones for blogger groups such as #lbloggers and #beautytalk. There are even very specific chats such as #rttc (responsible tourism Twitter chat).

You can search on Google and check out the Twitter profiles of influencers and high-level bloggers in your industry to see if there are relevant Twitter chats being hosted. As well as looking for great bloggers here, you can also join in with the chat if you have some valuable insight – a good move for getting your brand a little more exposure.

Search & Compare Users on Followerwonk and About.me: Followerwonk is a Twitter analytics tool provided by Moz. Followerwonk can be used to search Twitter bios, compare Twitter users, and analyse which users are the most influential. **About.me** (formerly known as WeFollow) is a similar tool which lets you find blogs and bloggers by topic and sort them by influence.

Using Facebook Groups to Find Influencers

Groups for Bloggers/Brands: There are a couple of Facebook groups where bloggers and brands can look for opportunities to work together. The most well known is the Blogger Opportunities group (facebook.com/groups/bloggeropportunities1), though it's mainly frequented by mummy bloggers and lifestyle bloggers.

Blogger Specific Groups: Many bloggers actively participate in Facebook groups related to their niche too. There are groups dedicated to very specific topics and although some of these groups have lenient admins, some of these groups will not approve membership to non-bloggers so check each group's rules. However, even if you are not a member you will be able to see who the admins are – more often that not, they'll be influencers in their blogging niche.

Resources & Tools for Finding Influencers

There are numerous tools out there, some free and others paid for, that will help you identify influencers. Unless you're running a massive influencers outreach campaign, it's unlikely that you'll need to invest in paid tools at this stage in the game as unpaid tools are pretty gangster as it is.

Blog Indexes: Similar to blogrolls, blog indexes are a list of the top bloggers – usually the top 100 – within a certain blogging niche. Not every niche has a blog index, but many of them do. A quick Google search should show you if there is one in the niche you're searching within. Two well known UK blog indexes are the Tots100 (tots100.co.uk), which features the top 100 mummy bloggers in the UK, and the HIBS100 (hibs100.co.uk), a list of the top 100 home and interiors bloggers in the UK.

Blog Discovery on Delicious: Delicious works like a personal search engine where you can search, collect and organise links. You can search blogs by tags in order to find blogs in particular niches and order them by the most popular or most recent links. It's also a good way to glean information on what topics are trending.

Blogs with "Viral Factor" on Digg, Reddit, and StumbleUpon: Digg, Reddit, and StumbleUpon are all content aggregator sites. These user-powered sites will pull up content which does well based on user votes so that you can see what kind of content gets shared from niche blogs.

Influencers on Bloglovin': Another content aggregator, Bloglovin' is more useful for finding high-end blogs and influencers. It's particularly popular within the fashion, beauty, and lifestyle bloggers, but all main blogging genres are searchable from the website's category buckets.

GroupHigh and Inkybee for Big Campaigns: Blogger outreach is time intensive, especially if you are manually researching and building lists of the bloggers you are going to contact. If you are going all out with a big campaign, then it may be worth investing in a tool such as **GroupHigh** and **InkyBee.** These are massive blogger search engines, blogger data spreadsheets, personalised pitch software, and campaign monitoring tools all rolled into one. **BuzzStream** is another useful software tool for managing larger campaigns.

Blogger/Brand Networks

There's been a rise in the number of blogger/brand networks. These networks are extensive blogger databases where brands can post campaign opportunities and be introduced by a digital PR middleman to relevant, targeted bloggers. They can save on the work, but a fee is usually required by the business.

We've just set up **ShoutOut.ly**, our very own blogger/brand network, so we totally recommend that one (because we know it's good). Other notable blogger/brand networks include Zeal Buzz, Bloggers Required, Joe Blogs Network, and the unimaginatively named The Blogger Network.

Ask Influencers You've Already Worked With

If you've already successfully collaborated with an influencer previously, then it's a great idea to ask if they know of any other influencers who would be interested in similar opportunities. Influencers are a tight-knit bunch, and so it's likely that they will be happy to send you a shortlist of their influencer friends who talk about similar topics and have a similar style. Plus, if you've got an influencer to vouch for you being a great business to work with to their friends, then you're more likely to secure some great partnerships with influencers in the future.

How to Measure Influence

By now you've probably got a bigger list of influencers than you know what to do with. To narrow down the best influencers to target, in order to get good returns on promoting your business, it's time to add some new columns to your influencer spreadsheet and look at some stats.

Blog Stats & Media Kit: Most bloggers who are open to working with brands will have a media kit or media pack available. A media kit will include all of the important stats about the blog, including monthly readers and social media followers, as well as previous brand work and their most popular blog posts. Bloggers may also provide their "Klout score." **Klout** is an online tool that ranks its users according to online social influence and gives them a score out of 100.

Here's a media kit for luxury travel and lifestyle blogger, Jasminne, who runs poshbrokebored.com:

Some bloggers may choose to simply write the stats on their "work with me" or "sponsor" pages. If you can't find a blogger's media kit or stats on their website, fire over a quick email and they should be happy to send it or their stats over to you.

Domain Authority (DA): DA is a measure of how likely a website is to rank well on search engines. The measurement is calculated based on the website's age, popularity, and size. The metric uses a 100-point scale, with 100 being at the top and 1 being the lowest. To give you an idea, The Guardian UK website is DA 97, while a new website I created yesterday is DA 1.

DA can be used to compare how "strong" websites are. You can find a blog's DA by searching the website URL on **Moz's Open Site Explorer**. Moz's OSE will also show you other stats, including how well pages on the website rank and how many other websites link to the blog.

Let's check out the DA for staceycorrin.co.uk, an amazing blogger who we've collaborated with on a number of very successful campaigns (please see top image on the next page).

Stacey's blog has a DA 31, which is a great score for a blogger. You can also see that she has an incredible number of links coming to her blog, which shows that lots of other websites like her content, and that she has a spam score of 0.

When working with small business clients on blogger outreach, we tend to look for bloggers who have a DA of about 20 up to about the DA 35-40 range. Beyond this kind of ceiling you'll often find that the bloggers are moving into the realm of A-listers, and their demands on small businesses can be far too high.

Keyword Rankings: Ideally you want to be working with blogs who are ranking well for the kinds of searches that you want your products or services to show up on. **SEM Rush** is a tool which allows you to plug in a blog's URL and check what the top organic keywords are.

Let's check out what keywords nomadicmatt.com, one of the leading travel bloggers, is ranking for:

live update **TOP ORGANIC KEYWORDS (158,146)**

Keyword	Pos.	Volume	CPC (USD)	Traffic
thailand travel	1 (1)	9,900	3.88	
nomadic matt	1 (1)	5,400	0.00	
central america	6 (6)	60,500	0.89	
travel blog	1 (1)	5,400	2.45	
angkor wat	10 (10)	49,500	2.22	

Export   View full report

Based on this we know that Thailand and Central America are the countries which Matt writes about that rank the highest and get the most interest from his readers. This means that a company working in either of those areas could make a massive impact if they secured an opportunity on Matt's blog.

Social Media Stats & Engagement: You'll want to make a note of how many followers or subscribers the blogger or influencer has on Facebook, Twitter, and any other relevant social media platforms such as Instagram or Pinterest. However, it's not all about the numbers. It's also about engagement. An influencer who has 10k Twitter followers that never like or comment on their social media updates is far less influential than someone who has just 2k Twitter followers that are engaged, interacting, and Retweeting their posts.

Check out Canadian blogger Amanda who runs fashion and lifestyle blog pinkthetown.com. She has just under 1,957 followers but her most recent contest Tweet has great engagement – 258 Retweets and 55 likes – which just goes to show how well a brand can benefit from collaborating with even a smaller-sized blogger.

I won't name any names, but compare this to a fashion and lifestyle who has over 12k followers on Twitter but next to no interaction on the majority of her Tweets:

It's easy to see from this comparison what an engaged audience can mean for a business partnering with a blogger. The more astute among us may have noticed that the four Tweets on this second blogger's Twitter profile look as though they may all be blog posts that involved brand partnerships – the words "review" and "wishlist" are dead giveaways.

Note: Facebook engagement and interaction are often quite low as a result of Facebook's changes to its reach algorithm. Social media experts have commented that Facebook is becoming more pay-to-play orientated.

Blog Post Engagement: Have a flick through some of the recent blog posts to see whether the blogger is getting comments from their readers. There is no hard science to this one as some blogs do not actively encourage users to comment on the blog post. Instead, they choose to engage in discussions about blog posts on Facebook or another platform. However, it is great to see users actively commenting and creating a discussion around a blogger's posts. It's even better to see the bloggers engaging with their readers in return.

Beyond the Stats...

Above all, what you actually want to do is find influencers that really resonate with you and your brand. There's no point working with an influencer whose content you're not that keen on just because they have a strong website DA and high follower numbers. Look for the best of both worlds and don't be afraid to experiment with who you work with. Sometimes you might find that the smaller guys put more work in because they appreciate the opportunity, and that's great for you.

> **Action Point: Create a list of 10 target influencers.** *Use the ninja search techniques above to find 10 influencers that would be a good fit to promote your brand. Consider the influencers' niches and how well their content style fits with your brand, as well as factors like their DA score, social media followers, and their followers' engagement. You will also need to collect contact information.*

Tip: You can often find a blogger's email address either on the sidebar, on their "about" or "contact" page, or on a "sponsor" or "work with me" page.

You may want to use a quick table or spreadsheet, as follows:

Blog URL	DA	Blogger Name	Email	Monthly Readers	Twitter Followers	Facebook Likes

Chapter 8

Connecting with Influential Bloggers in My Niche

Now that you know which influencers you want to work with, it's time to connect with them and pitch your brand. Before you dive in gung-ho and start throwing out emails, read our advice on connecting with and reaching out to bloggers.

In this chapter:

- 3 Simple Ways to Connect with Bloggers on Social Media
- What NOT To Do When Sending a Pitch Email to a Blogger
- Writing Blogger Outreach Emails that Make Bloggers <3
- What To Do If a Blogger Pitches to You
- How to Avoid #BloggerBlackmail Scandals (the Mutual Benefit Equation)
- Bonus Tips for Smashing Blogger Outreach!

There's an art to pitching and negotiating with bloggers, and part of that art is knowing what makes them tick. Before you even think about sending out emails pitching bloggers a giveaway with your product, make sure that what you're offering means they're getting as much benefit from running the competition as you are. Otherwise, you may as well just forget it now. How high profile the blogger is should factor into what you're offering.

If you're confident that the blogger is going to be getting a pretty sweet deal through working with you, then it's time to think about what you need to know to make this collaboration – whether it's a sponsored post, product review, giveaway, or something else – set the house on fire.

1. Check if the Blogger Has Run Product Reviews or Hosted Giveaways Before

See what kind of brand collaborations this blogger has done in the past. If a blogger has previously hosted a giveaway or run sponsored content, then it's more likely that they'll do it again. Some blogs will have a section specifically for reviews or giveaways, and on others you might have to use the search bar. See what products they've featured and whether yours match up or better them. If you can't find anything, that's not a dealbreaker. Sometimes bloggers will still be responsive to the idea of working with businesses, but use your noggin – think about the blogger's style and what opportunities they might be interested in.

2. Have They Written about a Competitor Before?

It's always worth knowing what your competitors are up to – and you can bet that the savviest among them have some kind of blogger outreach going on: whether that's sponsored content, sending out review products, or running giveaways. If you find a blogger has covered a competitor, then this is a good sign that they like products in this market and are willing to collaborate with brands. Even better, you can check how many post comments and social media shares were generated by the post to get an idea of the impact working with them could have for your brand.

3. Is their Content First Class?

The best results we've seen from competitions are thanks to bloggers who make a real effort with their blog content. A really good write up will get an audience excited, and that means they're going to be clicking to win! You don't want bloggers who are just going to throw any old thing up on their blog just for the free product. A blog post on "How to Create a Fantastically Colourful Kitchen (+ Coloured Mug Giveaway)" is much more captivating for readers than a blog post simply titled "Giveaway: Win Colourful Mugs". The better that blog post, the more likely you are to get lots of readers entering and sharing – and that means more exposure for your business.

Note: While bloggers will often want to write their own blog content, some will be happy for you to provide the blog post to feature because it means less work for them, it all depends on the blogger.

4. Do You Actually Like 'em?

This is probably the question that very few brands actually ask themselves! Do you actually like this blogger's content and style? Probably you do if they're still on your outreach list at this point. But once you've sent them an email, did you think their response was fair? Did they come across as likeable? You might go around badgering editors in order to get guest post content published, but when it comes to bloggers, you want to be working with responsive and efficient ones. If they're a hassle or make unreasonable demands in the beginning, that won't improve. In which case, cut yourself loose now. If they're lovely, crack on.

3 Simple Ways to Connect with Bloggers on Social Media

When you've got a shortlist of bloggers who you want to get in touch with, head to their social media profiles and give them a follow or a like. Don't leave it at that though. You also want to interact with them in some capacity so that they will notice your business' profile and will have a look around your company website. Here are some ways that you might do that:

"Like" some of their updates: Pick updates that you actually do like – don't just hit like on the first three posts you see. You want to look for updates and posts that resemble the kinds of interest your business and brand has.

Share or Retweet some of the posts: If there's a post that you think would resonate well with your own social media followers, then a really great way to get a blogger on board is to share or Retweet some of their content. Be selective here. You don't want to Retweet too many blogger's posts all in one go. This will clog up your Twitter profile, turning off both bloggers and potential customers.

Leave a comment: Ideally, you'd send the blogger a Tweet or leave a Facebook comment on a recent post. Steer clear of writing anything promotional about your brand though – this isn't an opportunity for you to advertise! Avoid any generic comments like "nice post" or "interesting topic" as well. Instead, try to add something valuable to the discussion. It's good to show your human side.

Don't be tempted to discuss opportunities for collaborating together over social media or on a public platform. If you Tweet that up in front of everyone and the blogger turns you down, it's not going to look great to your followers. Not to mention that sending 140 character messages is not the best way to convey any ideas about what working relationship you had in mind. You only want to use social media to put your business on the blogger's radar.

What NOT To Do When Sending a Pitch Email to a Blogger

When it comes round to emailing a blogger, you're going to need to invest a little bit of time in getting this right. There are lots of companies and digital PR folks (they're not ninjas) who are sending out lousy outreach emails. Lousy outreach emails will be an absolute flop, and so there's absolutely no point sending them out whatsoever. There's even less point paying someone to send them out for you.

While you may take more formal approach to corresponding with editors, bloggers tend to be more personable in their approach to collaborating with businesses. Sending out well-written and personalised emails to bloggers will garner positive, or at least polite, replies. Sending out press releases or blanket emails, on the other hand, will elicit negative responses or no reply at all. Before even thinking about sending an email to a blogger though, you should be sure you want to work with them. Get to know their blog style and the kind of content they write and connect with them on social media.

Let's take a look at some examples of blogger outreach emails and see what they did right – and more importantly, what some of them did wrong.

Blogger outreach email #1: unknown travel brand

> Dear Blogger,
>
> I am writing to you today about an opportunity to work with my brand. We'd be really pleased to let you work with us on our exciting opportunity relating to travel. We're sure that you and your readers will love our services! You can email me back and let me know if you are interested.
>
> Speak soon,

What They Did Wrong

- They have not said anything to show that they understand who the blogger is and what their blog is about.
- The blogger has no idea who they are. Not giving the name of the brand is suspicious stuff – is the brand awful? They don't trust the blogger enough to say who they are? Are they a secret underground organisation? It's also annoying as it requires an extra back-and-forth to establish key info.
- We have no idea what they're actually offering.
- They're very presumptuous – it's not likely the blogger will love their brand or that they'll speak soon with that kind of outreach email.

Blogger outreach email #2: branded shoe shop

> Hello,
>
> My name is ____and I recently began working with a shoe shop, called [brand name], that is attempting to increase their online presence.
>
> I came across your (_____.com) and think it would be a great fit for my client. They are looking for you to put a sponsored post on your website including a link back to their website.
>
> Please let me know if you have any information on your sponsored post rates.
>
> Sincerely,

What They Did Right

- They said the name of company – good, now we know who we're talking about and the blogger can look them up.
- It's brief and to the point.
- They are upfront about being prepared to pay the going rate.

What They Did Wrong

- Not personalised at all.
- Putting in the _____.com URL of the blogger's website instead of the name of the blog indicates that this is probably a generic email template.
- Asking for a "little link back" sounds a little bit weird, maybe some people can pull that off though.

Blogger outreach email #3: voucher for unknown business

Hi Jo!

I'm here to tell you about an amazing opportunity for bloggers like you — yes, you! — to get involved with our giveaway to win an amazing [product]!

Kick off the new year with £500 worth of [brand product]! Wow! Interested? To enter, post the attached image to your blog and make sure to link back to [brand website]!

Then ask your readers to follow the steps to enter. For each blog post you share, you will get additional two entries into the contest. If you post on Twitter, Facebook or Instagram and reference [social media account] you get another entry! If your readers share your blog post, you get even more entries! The blogger with the most entries wins!

What They Did Right

- Used the blogger's name – woohoo!

What They Did Wrong

- Why are they using so many exclamations marks!!!!!!!?
- It starts off very patronising as though they're doing the blogger a massive favour with this...
- What are they actually talking about? Looks like they're asking the blogger to give the company *free* promotion on their blog and then get readers to share it with only a very slim chance of winning.
- The blogger isn't guaranteed to get anything out of this competition, so there's not much benefit to them to put in the work.

Blogger outreach email #4: unknown travel brand

Hi Jo,

I just want to say that I LOVE, LOVE, LOVE your blog, its so, so amazing! I would love to work together in some way. What do you think? Do you have any ideas about how we can collaborate?

Looking forward to speaking with you,

PS. I followed you on Twitter too.

What They Did Right

- They used the blogger's name.
- They asked the blogger's opinion.

What They Did Wrong

- Their complements were so OTT that they seemed kinda fake.
- There's no information here whatsoever.
- It's good practice for the company to let the blogger know quite specifically about what opportunities are on the table and discuss from there. Open ended emails are hard to interpret.

You might think that these examples seem a bit extreme, but trust me here; they're not. There are plenty of people sending out pointless blanket emails like these to bloggers. A blogger will automatically delete an email if you do any of the following:

- Don't use their name – Dear Blogger or Dear Sir/Madam is not going to cut it here.
- Don't include an email subject – who is this spammer anyway?!
- Don't "reveal" your company name in the email – shifty, their company must be awful.

Successful blogger outreach is not about sending out emails to as many bloggers as you can, as fast as you can. There's software that does that, and guess what? It doesn't achieve anything.

Writing Blogger Outreach Emails that Make Bloggers <3

Now that you know what not to do, let's look at what you should do when sending a pitch email to a blogger. You should have hand-selected the bloggers who you want to approach and you should therefore tailor your pitch emails accordingly too. When you're emailing them, you should of course know their name, but you should have also read some of their recent blog posts.

A personable but professional approach is the way to go when you're emailing. Here's a foolproof structure for a concise, friendly and informative outreach email:

Start with:

Hi [name],

Introduce your company: One or two sentences should be enough to introduce your company and what they sell.

I'm writing to you on behalf of [company name], a unique yoga-wear brand. All of our yoga pants and clothing range are made from sustainable bamboo and the patterns are inspired by elements of the natural world.

A compliment: Say something nice but don't go OTT. If relevant, discuss a recent blog post or social media update that you liked on a personal level.

We're really fond of [blog name] and we thought your recent post on the hot yoga trend was really awesome. I'm into hot yoga myself and am just getting to grips with some of the postures you mentioned.

The opportunity: What are you going to give the blogger and what do you want in return? Make them an offer that is relevant to them, their blogging style, and their audience.

If you like our designs, [Company name] would love to send you a complimentary pair of yoga pants for you to feature on your blog. Would you be interested? Please have a look at our product range and let me know what you think!

Sign off: Keep it short and sweet.

Really looking forward to hearing back from you!

Kind regards,

Let's see that structure in action from a couple of different businesses:

Blogger outreach email #1: clothing brand

Hi Jo,

How are you? I'm currently working with Retro Fox Clothing and wanted to see if you would be interested in collaborating with us.

I've been checking out some of your autumn fashion blog posts on [Blog Name] and can see that you have some very stylish lookbooks which I think our clothing products could work really well in.

We would be happy to send out any of the following products for you to feature as part of a blog post and maybe a couple of social media posts:

- Dresses
- Jeans
- Winter boots

We'd like to ask for you to include at least 3 photos and link to [brand website] in the post. If this sounds like something you would like to go forward with, just let me know which clothing items you like most and the sizes you require!

Very best,

Blogger outreach email #2: travel company

Hi Ben,

Pleasure to e-meet you! I'm Jay and I'm working with Super Adventure Travel Tours, an adventure travel tour company who are based in Europe.

I can see from your awesome photos on social media (I loved that one of your dirt biking in Sierra Nevada!) that adventure travel is something you're passionate about.

We're asking our favourite travel bloggers to share blog posts on their top 10 travel destinations in Europe and what to do there. In exchange for mentioning us in the blog post, we'd be happy to provide a sponsored content fee or a discount to your readers.

Is this something you'd be interested in? If you could let me know by Friday so we can iron out some details, that'd be great.

Best regards,

Blogger outreach email #3: coffee seller

Hey Elle,

Ed here from Tiny Batch Coffee Co — we're a new, fair trade coffee seller on the market, buying green beans straight from the source and roasting them on-site in our own specialist roaster here in the UK.

I've been following your foodie adventures on [Blog Name] for a while now and I can see that you appreciate a good brew as much as I do. Perhaps you would be interested in trying out some of our coffee?

We'd love to send out a couple of bags of our coffee to you and get your opinion. If you like it, then it would be great to organise a giveaway on your blog so that your readers have the opportunity to win some as well. What do you think?

I've followed you on Twitter as well — and you can check out some of the stuff Tiny Batch Coffee Co get involved with.

Thanks,

What's great about these emails is that the companies who are writing them are friendly from the onset and give all the necessary information up front. Putting your offer on the table and being clear about what you would like in return not only shows the blogger that you're honest and easy to work with, but it also gives the blogger time to weigh up their thoughts.

What To Do If a Blogger Pitches to You

It's not unusual for bloggers to reach out to brands that they really like to see if there are any opportunities to collaborate. It's rare for bloggers to send their own pitches unless they really do personally like you're brand, so if you do receive one you should take it as a compliment!

However, it's still important to weigh up whether working with this blogger would be of benefit to your brand. Maybe they absolutely love your products and would like some free samples of your new product range for review, but perhaps their blog doesn't reflect quite how you want to position your brand? In this instance, the best thing to do is send an appreciative reply but politely decline their offer.

In some instances, you may like the blogger but feel their demands are too high to justify. It's absolutely okay to negotiate in a friendly and polite way with the blogger. Make them a counter offer and let them know what's feasible for your business. If the blogger sends an unfriendly reply, then they weren't worth working with anyway! More often than not though, the blogger will likely be happy to accept a lower offer.

The one thing you shouldn't do though is to try and get this blogger to promote your brand for free! This would be seen as cheeky, if not rude, by any blogger. Remember that any blogger contacting you is likely already a customer (or at least a potential customer!) so you should treat them with the same level of customer service as anyone else.

How to Avoid #BloggerBlackmail Scandals (the Mutual Benefit Equation)

When approaching influencers, you want to ensure that bothyou and the influencer are benefitting. You want to promote your products to a relevant audience who are going to see them and go "Oh, wow! I want that!" However, remember that influencers have spent endless hours building their audience and reaching like-minded people. They can be very protective of that fact. It takes time and effort to create a blog and build an audience, so bloggers won't want to take on any work that they don't feel they are really benefitting from.

If you were browsing on Twitter back in August 2015, you might've seen a trending hashtag #bloggerblackmail that went viral after a blogger and a business had a communication breakdown. The commotion started after a foodie blogger approached a London bakery for some free macaron samples in exchange for a review. Unfortunately, the blogger hoped to get quite a few more macarons for review than the bakery wanted to give away and *the situation exploded.*

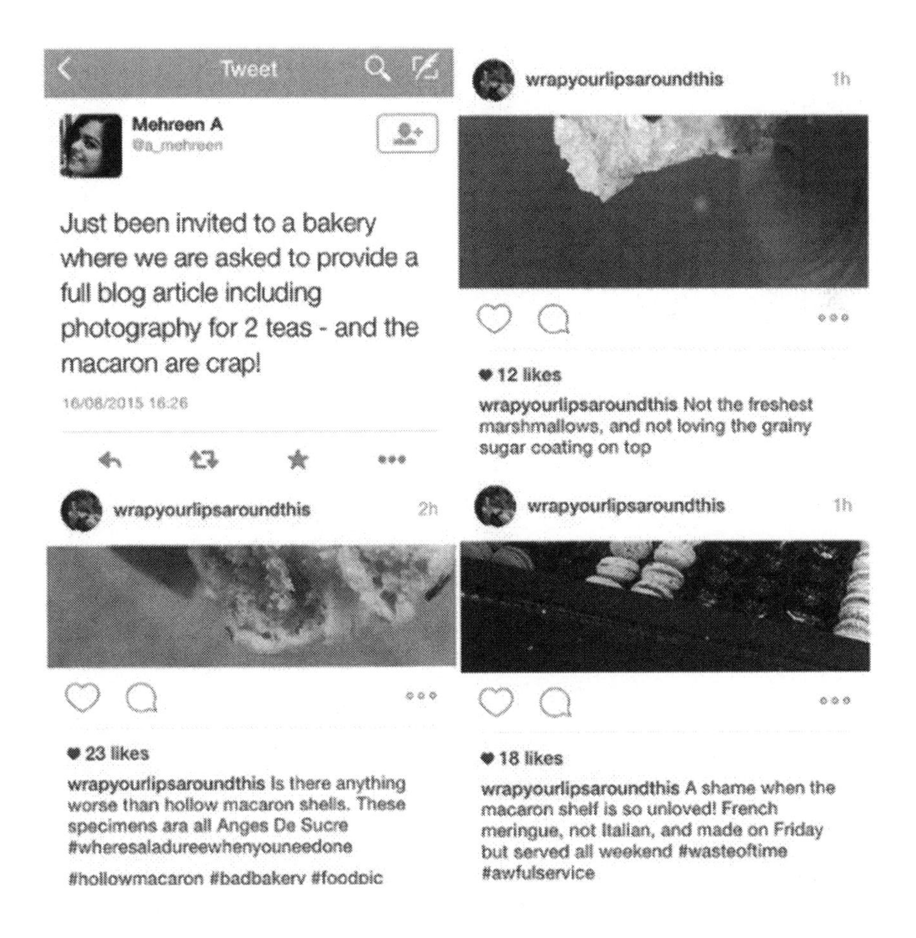

In response, the blogger made the very unprofessional decision to post some negative Tweets, Instagram updates, and a blog post about the situation with said bakery, which caused a huge backlash from others within the blogging community who said that this was "bad practice" (which it is) and felt that it reflected badly on the blogging industry as a whole.

Clearly expectations and reality didn't match up for the blogger or the bakery on this one. While the business clearly wouldn't be able to (and shouldn't) front the cost of the high demands for macarons from the blogger, the situation was definitely a result of a massive miscommunication between the blogger and the business. They both had different ideas about what would be a fair return for them and needed to set out clear expectations before any agreements were made.

Getting embroiled in a sticky situation like this doesn't benefit anyone involved – no business wants a bad review and no blogger wants to write one. It happens rarely, but the situation above goes to show that sometimes it does. Mess like this can be easily avoided by being selective about which bloggers you chose to partner up with and by agreeing on a mutually beneficial working relationship with a blogger beforehand. You can always negotiate in a friendly and informal way until you find a deal that works well for both of you.

What to Expect and How to Approach a Blogger

Here are four questions to ask yourself when reaching out to a blogger:

1. Is this blogger relevant to my brand?
You should be selective about which bloggers you choose to work with. Don't be tempted to send out a huge amount of stock to bloggers left, right, and centre. Instead, look for bloggers in a similar niche to your business who share

similar ideas and values. How can you tell what their ideas and values are? Have a quick read of their blog! The most effective blogger outreach work happens when everyone is working towards the same goal.

2. Are my expectations reasonable?
Businesses need to appreciate that bloggers put a lot of time and effort into building their blog and social media. Bloggers need to feel that the businesses are giving them enough for providing a review to be worthwhile and should never be asked to compromise their integrity by providing a "positive review."

3. Are the blogger's expectations reasonable?
Equally, bloggers need to be aware that businesses work hard to produce awesome products and services too. Businesses are the ones who have to front the cost to provide complimentary products and services, so it needs to be a fair exchange for you as well. If you feel that a blogger is being too demanding, politely withdraw your offer and move on.

4. Am I approaching this the right way?
Collaborating with bloggers can generate amazing exposure for your business, but always make sure that you're doing it the right way. Organising successful collaborations means putting in a bit of time to find bloggers who you genuinely would love to work with and corresponding with them to find an arrangement that benefits you both.

Bonus Tips for Smashing Blogger Outreach!

Get it in writing! We always recommend reaching out to bloggers by email and keeping a copy of the agreement which you came to during your conversations. Sometimes this might take a little back-and-forth, but it's worth it to avoid any undesirable situations and as a reference point for both you and the blogger.

Offer a little bit more. Getting coverage from bloggers is becoming increasingly competitive, especially in the beauty and fashion niche. The complimentary product or service is great and in some cases that will be enough, but if you can offer a little something extra to sweeten the deal then you're more likely to reach an agreement with the bloggers you'd really like to work with. Offering a preview of a product before release, offering a discount code that readers can use on your website, offering **affiliate links** for the blogger to use in their blog post, or sponsoring a giveaway are all awesome ways to increase your chances of getting fantastic coverage from bloggers.

Cultivate your relationships. Don't approach a blogger like you're entering into a formal business agreement where once it's through that'll be the end of it. When you approach them, be friendly and conversational. Even better, comment on their blog posts or join in discussions on their social media before reaching out to them. Don't be tempted to write spammy comments advertising your business or generic comments like "great post" either. Engage with what they're saying, ask questions, and leave insightful comments.

The result of well implemented product reviews or features where a business has partnered up with a very relevant and likeminded blogger, whose audience are genuinely engaged with the blogger's content, can be amazing. For just a free product, a one-off taster session, or something similar, you can gain some big returns at a low cost.

Chapter 9

Leveraging Product Reviews & Features by Bloggers

When potential customers type your business name or product name into Google, you want them to see your website followed by a whole list of good reviews. It can take years for new companies and small businesses to gain reviews, but you can speed the process up by sending out your products for review.

In this chapter:

- How Product Reviews Work — and Why You Should Get in on the Game
- 5 Super Awesome Benefits of Sending Out Products for Review
- Are Product Reviews Right for Your Business?
- Different Styles of Product Reviews — and When to Get Featured
- Product Reviews Go Hand-in-Glove with Social Media

If you're into your fitness, then you may have heard of blonde bombshell Faya, a personal trainer based in London and fitness blogger at fitnessontoast.com. She has 10k Twitter followers, over 20k Facebook followers, and an incredible 81.2k Instagram followers. Her blog is the 8th organic listing on the first page of Google for "fitness blog UK." Faya is what we could call a high authority blogger.

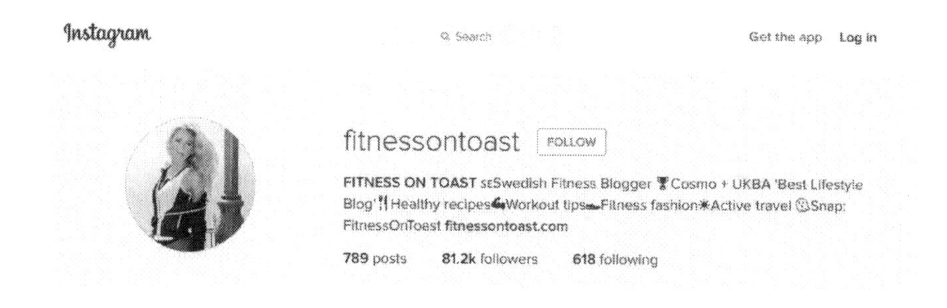

Let's check out some of her Instagram updates to get an idea of the style of content that she posts:

Are you starting to notice something? There is a certain sports shoe brand that's getting a lot of coverage on Faya's Instagram posts – and you can bet that this isn't just coincidence. While it may be the case that Faya just adores Nike and wants to spend all her shoe budget on Nike trainers, there's a more likely explanation for this. A little digging on her blog, pulls up this blog post:

OCTOBER 5, 2014

MY KIND OF NIKETOWN !!!

I recently went on **an active island escape/adventure hosted by Nike** – perhaps the most iconic and enduring of sports brands which, for me at least, conjures unforgettably powerful adverts of inspirational athletes deep from my childhood memories. Their eponymous slogan *Just Do It* was to become for me (and a wide collection of other bloggers) the ethos for the duration of our trip. **This post is a brief visual recap of that escape**, which also served to highlight the natural beauty of a (hitherto) completely undiscovered gem of an island – Sark in the Channel Islands. Click MORE to see it all

This is an example of a brand/blogger working relationship – Faya is regularly featuring Nike on her social media and blog because they have gifted her some complimentary trainers and, as we can see from the blog post above, hosted her as part of a blogger event to promote Nike.

Nike and Faya's individual brands fit really well together because they share a similar kind of audience, who – as we can see from the comments on the third Instagram post – are interested in and excited about the latest sports trainers for women.

If we check out Faya's disclaimer on fitnessontoast.com, we can see that she has a clear policy on which businesses and brands she choses to collaborate with and accept products from:

11) I am extremely keen that there should be no conflicts of interest on this site; I affiliate myself only with those products and companies I genuinely like, and by doing so, I am comfortable representing the merit I see in them to those who browse this site, or any of my social media accounts.

That's it really! Faya x

Fitnessontoast.com and Nike's blogger/brand relationship isn't an uncommon one. Check out these Instagram posts from Hannah Bronfman, Instagram influencer and fitness blogger behind hbfit.com:

Did you notice some brightly coloured Adidas trainers featuring in her posts? This is another example of a blogger/brand collaboration. Brands like Nike and Adidas are industry leaders thanks not only to their cool products, but to great publicity and coverage. Both Nike and Adidas know that being featured by relevant bloggers improves their clout (and klout), extends their reach to a relevant and targeted audience, and makes them look awesome.

It's not just fitness bloggers and sports brands who do this. If you start looking over the social media feeds and blog posts of bloggers in some different niches, you might start to spot some product placement going on. Maybe you've seen home bloggers featuring product roundups? How about beauty blogs with DIY tutorials including links to makeup brands that they love?

If I've said it before, I've said it a thousand times; I'm a spring and summer girl, through and through. I'm way happier when the sun is shining, and the garden is full of sweetpeas and delphiniums than when it's grey, raining and cold. That said, there is something nice about making the house cosy for the colder months; pulling blankets out of storage, finding the perfect pair of slippers and lighting a dozen tiny candles every evening. Today, I've got my top picks for warming up your home this autumn, from the comfiest chair to the best candles around.

1. Obligatory tea and a nice chunky mug

One of the best things about autumn and winter is searching out new tea; Ali and I discovered Bluebird Tea in Brighton when we went a few weeks ago, and we're hooked. Warming spicy blends are perfect for cold weather, an even more so if they're served in a beautiful handmade mug.

Spiced Pumpkin Pie Tea, Bluebird Tea Company: £ 5.70
Mali Dipped White Mug, Quince Living: £12.95

This product post was featured on home and lifestyle blog, theowlandtheaccordion.com.

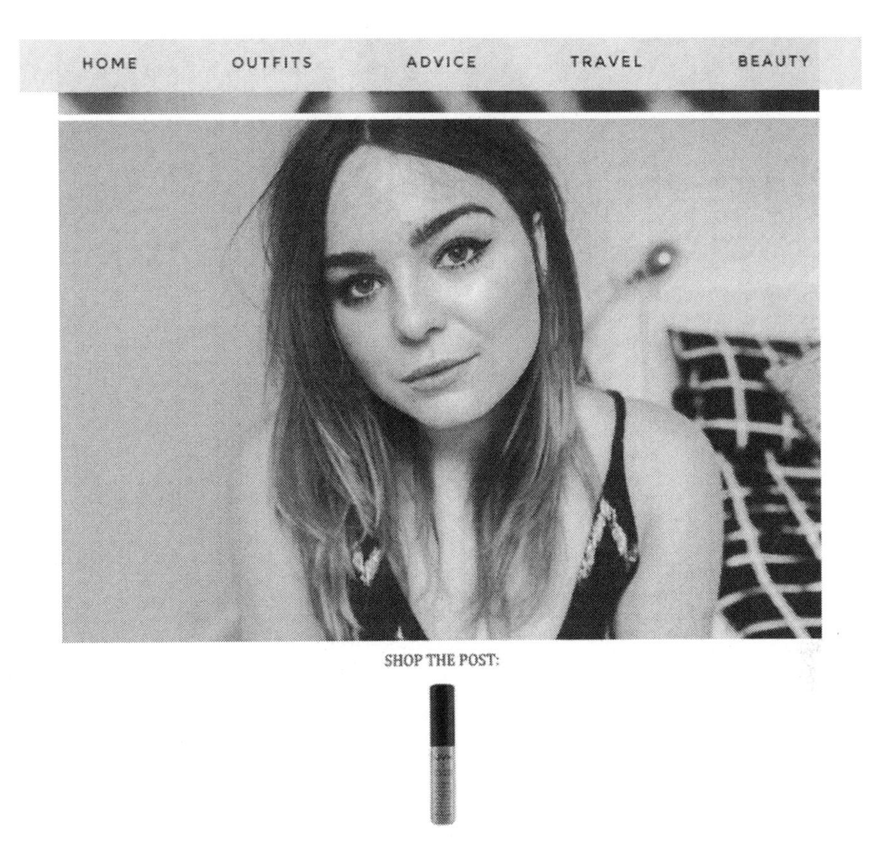

Lily from the beauty blog llymlrs.com features make-up from Selfridges in her blog post.

More often than not, these are **product features** have been arranged between brands and influencers. While these blog posts and social media updates might give the impression that the influencer just really wants to show off their fancy new Nikes and all the designer makeup that they love to treat themselves to all the time – which they probably do, to be fair – nearly all of these brand mentions are product reviews that are thanks to some pretty hard working digital PR folks.

It's not just the big brands who are collaborating with bloggers though; there are lots of small businesses using this strategy to promote their products. StressFreePrint, a small UK company who print business cards, leaflets, brochures, and other similar products, have collaborated with bloggers from various niches for product reviews of their business cards.

Ok so I know this isn't strictly travel related but now I am an award winning travel blogger (no I don't think I will get bored of saying that, although I may stop going on about it soon) I needed to get some business cards as they are such an essential item for a blogger and I always have some in my bag. I have had some in the past but I really needed a lot in time for visiting The Family Travel Show in October and World Travel Market in November.

When StressFreePrint offered to send me some business cards and help me design them, I quickly said yes please. The service I received from Stress Free was fab. I sent them some images and they designed them for me. I wasn't keen on the first design, and I tweeked the second, and in the end I think we ended up with the fourth design. Each time Gavin

StressFreePrint's business cards featured on Mini Travellers, a respectable authority blog about travelling with kids, in a product review.

StressFreePrint are a lovely bunch of really helpful people and nothing is too much. Prices start at only £29.99 for 1000 business cards and putting together your order online is really simple - as long as you haven't lost your artwork! They can print onto virtually any size or shape you wish, including stand up cards, and have a range of finishes and papers including recycled.

As well as business cards they print just about anything. A1 posters start from only £2.49 and A3 leaflets from £48 per 1000, and 50 Christmas cards with your own design and words printed on recycled paper would cost you less than £62. Having the designers create your image for you adds around an extra £50, which is very fair price for a professional's time and ideas, and they do a great job.

My business cards were created and sent to me free of charge for review.

Their business cards also featured on The Brick Castle, a mummy blog of a similar authority to Mini Travellers, in another review of their service.

Meridian, who sell organic, palm oil-free nut butters and similar healthy food products, have run a more targeted campaign. They have been collaborating with natural and whole food bloggers on features and recipe based posts.

Meridian Nut Butters

As many of you will know I am a crazy nut butter fan so when I was offered some Meridian nut butters to review I couldn't say yes fast enough! I tried the smooth cashew, almond and peanut butter and all three are utterly delicious. What I really love about Meridian is that their products are 100% nuts with nothing added. I love the amazing texture of them as well. It's fabulous that these are now available in general supermarkets as well as specialist health food stores. The only way I can fault these is that the oil in the peanut butter always seems to leak out a little, but that's nothing a kitchen towel can't fix. These are without a doubt a healthy kitchen cupboard staple!

Find out more about Meridian products on their website, Facebook and Twitter.

This blog post from Naturally Sassy, a small but well respected recipe blog with 3,000 Twitter followers, features Meridian cashew nut butter in a smoothie recipe.

Meridian also featured on Whole Heartedly Healthy, a higher authority blog with more sizeable social media followings, in a health and beauty product roundup.

It just goes to show that you don't need to be Nike or Adidas to run a successful product review campaign with bloggers. Blogs come in all shapes and sizes and there will be a blogger out there to suit your brand, no matter how small or large, how weird or wonderful.

How Product Reviews Work — and Why You Should Get in on the Game

Influencers create content that their followers love – whether that's blog posts on their website, videos on YouTube, or photos on Instagram – and because of that they hold a lot of influence over people's buying habits too. While traditional TV advertisers are still using celebrity names like Kiera Knightley to advertise Chanel perfume and Kate Moss to advertise Rimmel lipstick, the online generation look to bloggers they love and trust to recommend products and services.

The world is moving beyond TV advertising and towards online advertising. As many as 60% of UK shoppers consider themselves to be highly capable when it comes to researching and purchasing products online. This shift towards online shopping has led to a rise in the number of people researching products and services before buying online, and quite often this will lead them to product reviews written by bloggers.

> 61% of online consumers are reported to have made a purchase based on recommendations from bloggers.
> Figures from BlogHer

Blogs are more trusted resources for shoppers than any of the social media platforms. Bloggers who have a truly engaged readership have a lot of influence: their readers trust what they say, take their advice to heart, and buy products that they recommend. It's the same for any other influencer and their audience, whether they are a YouTube sensation or an Instagram star.

This is great news for small businesses who are looking for ways to promote their products or services online. Collaborating with bloggers and other influencers to promote your product can be a highly effective way of building trust in your brand and getting those all important sales coming through.

If you're still teetering on the edge with whether you feel it's worth sending out review products to influencers, then think about the following benefits for your business:

1. Strengthen Brand Trust and Recognition

It's good to have a continual, positive buzz surrounding your products. Collaborating with bloggers is a great way to do that and sending out review products shows you're confident in your product, that you believe it's awesome, and that in turn makes people more confident about buying from you.

Getting good reviews and being featured by bloggers and other influencers helps to build trust in your brand. The more times your products or services are mentioned and viewed online, the more recognisable your brand becomes. This in turn builds trust with consumers – we trust the brands we recognise. Think Apple, Sony, Argos, or Costa Coffee.

2. Build Backlinks Quicker

If you're main goal here is to build links and improve your own website rankings, then you'll want to focus on working with bloggers. Product reviews are far more efficient than guest posting when it comes to building links. If you don't already have industry contacts, then building relationships with editors, following up on your correspondence, and writing up truly valuable articles to suit each publication in order to secure a publication with a backlink takes up a huge amount of time. A product outreach strategy allows you to build backlinks quicker.

Bloggers are way, way more likely to agree to product reviews than guest posts and the blogger will nearly always take care of writing the article. Bear in mind though that Google's guidelines warn against directly paying for links that pass PageRank and this should not be part of your negotiation with a blogger. You shouldn't being going crazy sending out products to just any influencer or being spammy about trying to build links here. This kind of outreach works better when you are selective about which bloggers would best represent your brand.

3. Reach a Relevant Audience, Connect with Like Minded Influencers

It's awesome for new brands to connect with influencers who truly love their products. Building a relationship with an influencer not only means that you are able to reach out to a new and relevant audience through them, but it can also help to establish connections within influential blogging circles. That, and an initial small collaboration with a blogger, might lead to repeat promotion from them if they really did enjoy working with you and liked your products.

All of the best collaborations come from brands who have found bloggers that have the same values and beliefs as their company. Take a business who sells bespoke handbags for example – while there might be lots of great travel blogs out there, it's just not something those bloggers would be interested in. Reaching out to high-end fashion bloggers and social media stars would be a much better means of connecting with influencers that really love the product.

4. It's Cheaper than Running Ads

70% of online consumers learn about companies through articles like blog posts, not from ads. Not to mention that the cost of banner ads or sponsored content on other websites can be sky high. Product reviews are a much cheaper way of building links to your website and getting your products noticed.

Sending out a product for review, in many cases, will only set you back the cost price of a product plus the postage. Some bloggers may ask for small hosting fees, depending on the authority of their blog. If you've got a £12.99 product and postage costs you £2.99, then £16.98 is a totally ninja deal for a blog post featuring your product and potentially linking back to your website.

5. Create a Buzz on Social Media

Be sure to connect with any influencers you're working with on Facebook, Twitter, Instagram and any other relevant platforms. Many powerful bloggers will have hundreds, if not thousands of followers, and social media influencers will have an even more targeted and loyal social media following, allowing your brand to be seen by an entire cohort of like minded people.

Influencers often work in networks, reading each other's blogs and engaging in conversation via comments and social media. Targeting a particular blogger niche allows your brand to be seen organically by interested readers.

If you get involved with sharing content as well, this is a great way to create a buzz across social media platforms.

It's worth remembering that people will view social media statistics as evidence for a brand's "trustworthiness". The higher the number of followers that regularly engage with the brand, the more trustworthy they are thought to be. Whereas a low number of unengaged followers implies people aren't interested in your products and don't trust your brand.

Are Product Reviews Right for Your Business?

It's fair to say that product reviews aren't right for every business. However, for the ones that they are relevant to, they can have a huge impact. To know, answer these two questions:

Do you run an e-commerce site?

Yes? Bang on the money. Product reviews work best for businesses who run e-commerce sites and especially those who have lower ticket items that mean the cost of sending out products is lower. These products could be anything from home accessories and kids' clothing to screen protectors and yoga mats.

If no, then...

Are you service based business?

Product reviews can also be relevant for service based businesses. For example, if you run a beauty salon, why not invite local lifestyle and beauty bloggers in for a complimentary facial or nail treatment? If you're a photographer, maybe you could offer free 30-minute photo shoots to fashion influencers to feature on their Instagram accounts? If you're a personal trainer, then how about providing free fitness consultations or one-off sessions for health vloggers?

If you answered yes to one of the above questions, then ask yourself the following questions to know if product reviews could be a beneficial PR route for your business:

- Would my product/service appeal to influencers?
- If so, which kind of influencer? (e.g. blogger, vlogger, Instagrammer)
- In which niche? (e.g. lifestyle, design, beauty, mummy, fitness)
- How many products could I feasibly send out for free?

If you can identify a target audience for your products within popular influencer niches and are able to shoulder the cost price of the products, then arranging product reviews and features with influencers can work super well for your business. Do you feel like you could be onto a winning strategy here? You could be right, but you need to make sure that you're approaching the right influencers and gaining the right kind of product reviews in order for them to really benefit your business' online presence and sales.

Different Styles of Product Reviews — and When to Get Featured

Let's say you're after product reviews on blogs, which will be the route most small businesses take. Every blogger has their own style of content and each will approach product review posts from a different angle. Product reviews come in a variety of different formats, ranging from straight up review articles and product roundups to Christmas gift guides and more covert features. There are many factors that affect the kind of product review that bloggers create, including the niche/industry, their content style, the value/size of the item, how much information they have about the product/service, the time of year (i.e. Christmas time means more gift guides are being written), and so on.

Instead of going all out and writing a complete advert about your product – which very rarely happens – it's much more likely that a blogger will review a product or service by showing their readers how your product fits into their lifestyle as part of a product review or feature. That might be a lipstick they use on Friday nights, a peanut butter that they use in their recipes, or their favourite leggings for yoga practise.

If you have particular requirements about the kind of content that you would prefer, you can definitely discuss that with the blogger. Though many bloggers will already have their own preferences here, they will also be open to ideas and suggestions for the blog post. Here are some scenarios of when and how various companies might decide to approach bloggers:

Scenario #1: Got spare rooms in your your hotel during the winter months?

Instead of letting January pass by with unoccupied rooms, invite bloggers along to review your accommodation. This is the perfect opportunity for you to gain reviews without losing out on bookings during high-season. This is exactly what we did with our client, a boutique hotel based in a historic city in south west of the UK, to generate some extra coverage and exposure for them during quiet times. They gained reviews from some of the best UK lifestyle bloggers and they were even featured in the high end House of Coco magazine.

Glamping company, Canopy & Stars, did the same thing:

Generator Hostels did it too:

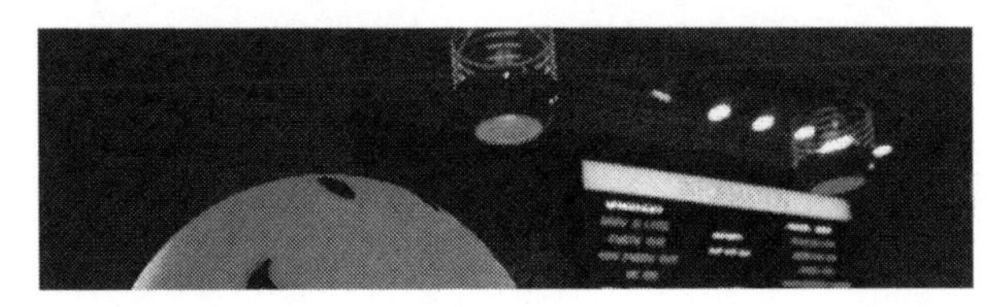

Scenario #2: Are sales for your really awesome rucksack lower than you'd like?

Imagine you're a company selling rucksacks for travellers. The summer holidays are coming up and you want to get some attention for and get a sales boost for a particular product that's not selling as well as you'd like. Featuring your backpack on influential travel blogs will mean that plenty of would-be travellers will be eyeballing your products right before the travel season begins.

This backpack from Farpoint40 was featured in a review post by popular travel bloggers Never Ending Voyage:

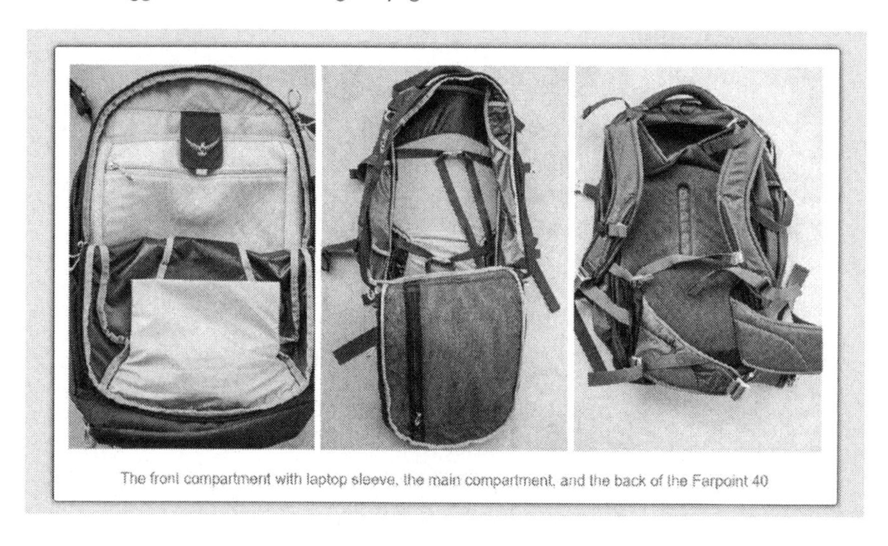

A number of different rucksack brands featured in Snarky Nomad's "best travel rucksacks" blog post:

Scenario #3: Would your product make the perfect Christmas stocking filler?

If you have lower ticket items that would make for great stocking fillers at Christmas, then being featured in Christmas gift guides by relevant bloggers could result in increased sales during the festive season. We had fantastic results with sending out products to feature in Christmas gift guides for an e-commerce client who sells retro homewares, including mugs, glass jars, and mixing bowls. Christmas gift guides are popular across various niches, and they work really well for e-commerce websites selling smaller items.

For example, here's a Christmas gift guide for children from a London-based mummy blog:

1. Knitting dolls to keep idle hands busy! 2. Fearsome slippers

3. Mini accordion – excellent gift for anyone who doesn't actually live with the little! Ideal from aunts and uncles. Drum kits also an excellent option.

4. Mini country play kitchen 5. Ride on racer (in British racing green) 6. Old school bike

This alternative Christmas gift guide is from a feature on an eco-green blog who promote ethical products:

1. Pocket Knife (£40.00) by Trevor Ablett via The Future Kept. This beautiful knife is handmade by Sheffield based Trevor, and perfect for the outdoors type..

2. Harris Tweed Wallet* (£24) by Life Covers via Etsy UK - made using Harris tweed.

3. Griffin Woodtones Headphones* (£24.99) from Ethical Superstore - a slightly more environmentally friendly way to enjoy your favourite music.

4. Thug Kitchen Cookbook* (£10.46) from Wordery - everyday vegan recipes with an extra side of swear words!

If you know that you're going to have vacant rooms, leftover stock of a discontinued item, particular products you want to promote, or if there's a time of year when you could do with the extra sales boost, then plan ahead. This way you can organise product reviews and social media coverage with bloggers at the best time for your business.

Note: No matter what kind of review or feature the blogger is writing, if they are following FTC regulations then the blogger should include a disclaimer to say that the blog post was sponsored by or that the products were supplied by the brand.

Product Reviews Go Hand-in-Glove with Social Media

Bloggers will nearly always share their blog posts and product reviews on their social media channels. The exception to this will be the A-Listers (the very high authority bloggers) who charge different rates for blog posts and social media promotion. If you're working with high ranking bloggers, be sure to clarify expectations before sending out any products or giving away your services.

However, the majority of bloggers will share their content of their social media channels and this means that there's also a lot of opportunity for businesses to gain some coverage here as well. If you have a good blogger/ brand match, responses from social media can be really good. Quite often, you'll also see numerous comments from readers who love the products that have been featured on these blog posts as well as heart-eyed emojis on the blogger's social media status updates.

Hannah Bronfman's new shoes got a whole bunch of those emojis, not to mention those 4000 likes:

Lifestyle and mummy blogger, Lori, behind the very beautiful Wild & Grizzly blog, Tweeted about her stay with glamping Company Canopy & Stars. She tagged the company in the Tweet and they responded by both liking and Retweeting her post. It was also Retweeted and liked by other lifestyle bloggers:

Businesses who collaborate with bloggers should follow, interact, and engage with bloggers on all of their social media platforms. Many businesses can be tempted to let their social media fall by the wayside and instead focus on just getting a review post about their product from bloggers. But a little effort can go a long way! If you're friendly on social media, then bloggers will be friendly in response, and this will mean extra exposure for your brand. Interacting on social media is part of building relationships with bloggers. The more effort that you put into it, the more you will get in return from the bloggers.

Chapter 10

Running Competitions & Giveaways with Bloggers

Build backlinks, boost your social media followings, and reach new customers with giveaways.

Take your digital PR work with blogger one step further by running competitions and giveaways to really capitalise on blogger influence.

In this chapter:

- The Power of "Free" Stuff (and Why You Should Be Running Giveaways)
- The 3 Ingredients of a Giveaway that's Irresistible to Readers
- Getting Your Hands Dirty (How to Run Your First Competition)
- How to Set Up Rafflecopter: in Just 10 Steps!
- Going Big Time! Running Multiple Giveaways All in One Go

Imagine that you're a small business selling glass jars. You can store herbs and spices in them, put candles inside to make pretty tea lights, or use them as funky cocktail vessels. E-commerce sites selling home and kitchenwares are overflowing with similar products because they appeal to a wide market. How do you get your little glass jars noticed in such a crowded marketplace?

- Run an ad campaign – but is £1 per click really worth the spend?
- Try and get your website to the top of Google for the phrase "glass jars" – that's not going to happen overnight.

- Send out a product for review? I think we can do one better!
- Collaborate with a blogger to run a giveaway – bingo!

And that's just what we did. We researched a shortlist of amazing lifestyle bloggers that fitted in really well with the brand of the business selling the glass jars, and we checked out their social media numbers too. We sent out a few emails asking if the bloggers would like to use a set of glass jars as a prize for a giveaway to readers of their blog. We heard back from one of the best bloggers on our shortlist. She excitedly agreed and set about writing a blog post on creative ways that these glass jars would be used around the home to feature alongside the giveaway, including a little backlink as thanks to the company for providing the glass jars.

The competition required people to like, follow, and Retweet the glass jar company's Facebook and Twitter pages to gain entries. Within just 10 days, the competition received an incredible 3,000+ entries. It also gained the company 300 new Twitter followers and 150 Facebook likes. The total cost of the contest was the £12.50 retail price of the product. That's a lot of bang for your buck, right?

The power of this contest was not only in finding the right product to offer, but positioning it in a way that made people *really* want it. That fab blog post showcasing how these jars could be transformed into amazing interior pieces, gorgeous gifts, and handy storage solutions meant readers were much more inclined to enter the contest. Much more so than if it was simply promoted from the business' own page or on a blog that didn't have the audience engagement of the one we worked with.

Exposure to this sort of audience is exactly what the company needed from social media. Working with a blogger in a relevant niche meant that this business was able to tap into and appeal to an audience that hadn't heard of

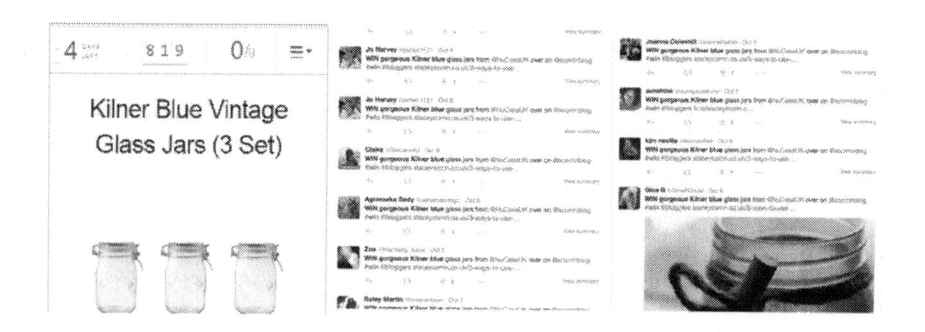

them before. It's just like being the new kid on the playground: on the first day no one even knows your name, but once you've made friends with the cool kid and handed out a couple of sweets, others start talking about you and soon it turns out that you're pretty popular too.

The Power of "Free" Stuff (and Why You Should Be Running Giveaways)

People like free stuff. It's true, and we all know it. It may be embarrassing to admit it, but when when we hear the word "free" roll off of someone's tongue, suddenly our ears prick up. There's an almost irrational pull from knowing that something is free. As long as we perceive the value of the free thing to be high enough, we'll bend over backwards to get it. Successful businesses have long known this, and they have long used it to their advantage.

Take the famous Hershey's experiment. They started of selling chocolate at a discounted price. Hershey's Kisses costed something around the 5p mark and Lindt truffles were priced at 20p. The higher quality Lindt chocolate was more popular, not only because it tasted better but because it was a better deal (at full price the Hershey's was worth 20p but the Lindt truffle was worth £1). Next, the experimenters dropped the price of both chocolates drops by 5p. The Hershey's Kiss was now free, while the Lindt truffle costed 15p. What happened? Almost everyone chose to have the free chocolate! Logically, this doesn't make sense because the premium Lindt truffle was still worth more and therefore a better deal.

The power of free was too strong though – despite having proven that people prefer the Lindt chocolate and despite it offering better savings, people assign an additional value to stuff that is free. There are many ways that you can put this knowledge to good use and running a giveaway is one of them. Household names like Yankee Candle, Amazon, Huggies, Forever21, Aeropress and Canon are just a few of the big brands who run giveaways with bloggers and influencers. All of these products are very different and therefore naturally have a different target audience, but each of them are able to tap into a particular blogger niche to reach new consumers to gain traction on social media.

The glass jar example has shown us that you don't need to be a big brand to make a big impact with your products through blogger giveaways. We've successfully run giveaways featuring a whole array of products from various small businesses and startups, including mixing bowls with foodie bloggers, LED keyrings for kids with mummy bloggers, and unique art prints with home design bloggers. As long as you're able to find and collaborate with relevant bloggers, be they lifestyle, design, beauty, fashion, travel, mummy, tech or any other niche of blogger, then you can reap the benefits of running a product giveaway.

Like product reviews, giveaways have the benefits of gaining exposure for your business, strengthening brand trust and recognition, building relationships with relevant influencers, securing backlinks quicker, and being cheaper than running ads. However, the benefits don't end there! Unlike sending products for review, running giveaways also allows you to do these three awesome things:

1. Build an Email Database

Not everyone who lands on your website will convert straight away. People need time to think about purchases. Growing an email database of newsletter subscribers is a good strategy to remind customers about your products and increase conversions. When running a giveaway, an input email function allows you to collect email addresses and entrants can opt in to be subscribers. Newsletters can be sent out with product info and special offers on a regular basis. This constantly reminds potential customers about your brand and your awesome products, while boosting their trust in your brand and eventually leading to a sale.

2. Create a SUPER Buzz on Social Media

While product reviews will gain you will get a few people sharing and Retweeting, product giveaways will get A LOT of people doing so. Giveaways are a dead cert to increase your own social media followers, get shares and Retweets, and get some website hits. By collaborating with a blogger, you get to tap into their social media following too and get them engaged with your product. Hashtags can be effectively used to gain exposure for the competition and your products in turn.

3. Promote Your Website

It's common courtesy for a blogger to link back to your website on the competition page where the giveaway is being hosted to let readers know the source of the product (just like a product review would). Still, what's even better is that by giving away a product, you're showing that you really have faith in how good your stuff is. And so is the blogger! Having someone promote your product like this is awesome for business.

Note: If you decide to a host a competition on your own website, you can link through to the relevant product page in order to drive traffic in that direction. Holding a competition on your own business website is only recommended for businesses who already have strong social media followings and online clout.

The 3 Ingredients of a Giveaway that's Irresistible to Readers

There are only three ingredients to creating a spot on giveaway that gets killer results for your business:

1. A Tasty Product

Without something sufficiently tasty, even making it free won't be enough to elicit a response. This type of contest needs a good level of response to take off, so if in doubt offer more. Don't attach strict conditions, postage, or anything that removes the "free" perception. The product doesn't have to be particularly expensive, but the audience does have to want it with sufficient desire.

If you sell products, we've found that inexpensive but versatile items tend to do best. Think of something with mass appeal and various uses. If you're a service business, again it's important to offer something that a large percentage of your audience is likely to value. Also **consider giving away a voucher** with a monetary value in a giveaway. This will encourage entrants to start browsing around your website to see what kind of products or services they would be able to get in exchange for that amount. If you have a lot of appealing products, this can be a very tempting offer!

2. A Hungry Audience

You'll see a marked improvement in your contest's response if you partner with a blogger or publication that already has a hungry crowd. Look for bloggers whose audience engages with them on social media and on blog post comments.

Don't be afraid to ask the blogger's opinion on what sort of prize will be likely to draw a response either. They should know their audience well and have a good feeling for how to get them to respond. If they have feedback or suggest a different angle, we'd suggest considering it seriously. The more appealing the prize, the more they are likely to share and promote it. Remember that, by giving away a decent prize, they raise their own value in their audience's eyes so they'll be more willing to share across different channels and run follow up posts.

3. Easy Entry Method

The most successful contests are those that are simple to enter. Asking someone to like a page, share something, Retweet something, or comment on a post will more likely generate entries than asking people to submit the email addresses of 5 friends or asking them to send in pictures. The latter strategies can be useful for higher-value contests. Though, to generate maximum engagement, keep it simple. I'd recommend using a giveaway widget which lets people enter the competition really easily. Among the most popular and easy-to-use giveaway widgets are **Gleam, Wildfire,** and **Rafflecopter**.

One final tip! Remember that if you're asking people to like a Facebook page or follow a Twitter account, they'll be visiting that page during the contest. It needs to look buzzing, so don't send them through to a tumbleweed profile with no cover photo or you'll be shooting yourself in the foot. Once they're a follower, make sure that they're seeing valuable and relevant content from you or they'll unfollow and the long-term benefits of the contest will be lost.

Getting Your Hands Dirty (How to Run Your First Competition)

So, you've successfully reached out to some cool bloggers who are on board and ready to run a product giveaway with you? Awesome. Now, you need to organise the competition, and you'll be pleased to hear that it's as easy as pie once you know how.

Once the blog post is taken care of – either by you or by the blogger, depending on your agreement – you'll need to embed a giveaway widget which lets people enter the competition. We mentioned before that popular giveaway widgets include Gleam, Wildfire, and Rafflecopter.

The easiest and cheapest to use is Rafflecopter, and it's used by a whole heap of digital PR companies who set up competitions for their clients (including us). We always recommend Rafflecopter for clients who are keen to use a giveaway to a) get more subscribers to their mailing list, b) make a big impact on social media, or c) both of those things.

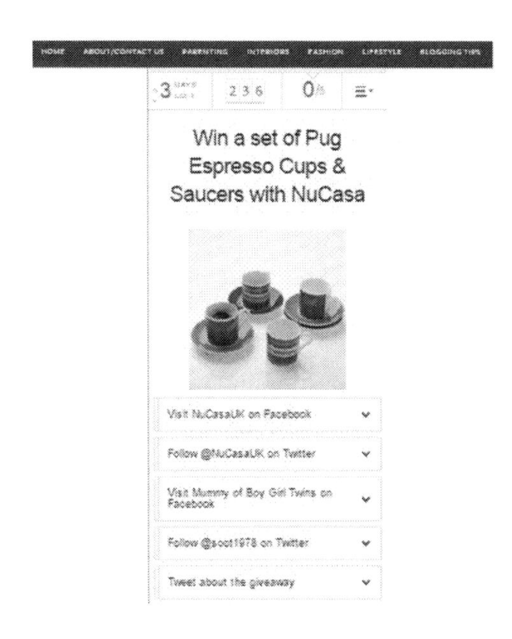

By using social contest software such as Rafflecopter, it's possible to measure engagement statistics and manage large contests with the bare minimum of admin hassle. It tracks entries and allows people to enter multiple times by completing social "tasks" such as liking, following, and Retweeting.

How to set up Rafflecopter in just 10 steps!

1. First of all, head over to rafflecopter.com and sign up for a basic account.
2. Click on "add a new giveaway" and follow the instructions to set it up. These are quite straightforward but if you're unsure there are some useful resources on Rafflecopter's website.
3. Use the product name in the prize field, such as: "Win this awesome [product] from [company]!"

4. Upload a high-res, cool-looking photo of your product for the widget image.
5. Decide how you want people to enter the competition. Readers can enter in different ways, such as following you on Twitter, sending out a Retweet about the competition, signing up to your newsletter, and so on. They can earn extra points by entering in multiple ways. Decide what would work out best for you based on your business goals and select accordingly. Don't forget to include options to enable entrants to follow the blogger on Twitter and to view their Facebook page as well as your own.
6. When selecting "Tweet about Giveaway", be sure to include your business' and the blogger's Twitter handles. The widget will automatically pick up the URL of the page that the widget is embedded in, so don't worry about that. Add in the #win hashtag and any other relevant hashtags.
7. Select how long you want the competition to run for. This is really entirely up to you. Many businesses choose to run short and sweet competitions of around 10 days to create an immediate hype and get the ball rolling right away. If you're running a competition leading up to a launch date or an event like Christmas or Valentine's, then you might want to extend the run time to get more entrees the closer it gets to the big event.
8. Add in the Terms & Conditions. Rafflecopter has a template for this to make life easier. Be sure to specify which countries the giveaway applies to and if there are any age restrictions with who can enter.
9. Preview the widget. Check that the design will fit in okay with the design/ colours of the blog where it will be embedded. The last thing that the blogger will want is clashing colours!
10. You're all done! Copy the embed code of the widget and send to the blogger via email so that they can add it into their blog post.

What to Do When the Giveaway Starts: Make a Note & Promote

Just before the giveaway is about to go live, **make a note** of the number of Twitter followers, Facebook likes, and other relevant stats for your business' social media pages. This way, when the giveaway finishes you'll be able to see the increase. The number of giveaway entries will be displayed on the Rafflecopter widget.

PROMOTE! This one's a biggie. You want to get as much traction for your competition as possible and that means you need to get your hands dirty with some social media promoting. Ideally, you want to be Tweeting about the giveaway every day and sharing an update on Facebook every couple of days. Don't forget to add in the URL of the competition, tag the blogger so that they can Retweet, and add an image to get people clicking. Experiment with a couple of different hashtags, including the obvious ones like #win, #giveaway, and #FreebieFriday to reach more people.

You may also want people to Retweet and share with a specific competition hashtag so that you can keep track of social media entrants. This could simply be something along the lines of #[brandname]giveaway. You'll want to include an eye catching image with some easy to read text about your giveaway when posting to social media. You can use **Canva** (canva.com) to add text and create more attractive images.

If you're social media savvy, then you can schedule all your posts in one go by using a tool like **Buffer** (buffer.com) or **Hootsuite** (hootsuite.com) to schedule Tweets.

What to Do When the Giveaway Ends

Fortunately, Rafflecopter has made this part a breeze too. When your giveaway ends, you'll get an email through from Rafflecopter. Simply follow the link and click to randomly select a winner. Rafflecopter will give you the winner's name, email address, and Twitter handle if they have one.

Email them with a *Congrats!* and ask for their address so that you can send the product right on over to the lucky reader. If you have their Twitter handle, then send out a final tweet about the competition congratulating them as well.

Send a follow up email to check that they've received and are happy with their product. You can also ask them to share a photo of them putting their new product to work with you on social media as this is another great way to signal to your followers that people love your products.

Going Big Time! Running Multiple Giveaways All in One Go

If you're feeling confident about running giveaways with bloggers, or have enlisted some digital PR and social media help and have a higher budget available, you can consider running giveaways with multiple bloggers all at once.

Houseology, an online interior design store selling designer furniture and lamps, teamed up with a group of influential home interiors bloggers to run multiple giveaways where all of the bloggers linked up their blog posts to one another. Each blogger was given a £500 voucher to give away, but each voucher was for a slightly different set of products, therefore encouraging readers to click through and enter each of the competitions.

WILD & GRIZZLY

I'm Lori, mama to a boy named F. This is a place where mama meets cool. For lovers of design, travel, style and interiors while exploring the wilds of motherhood.

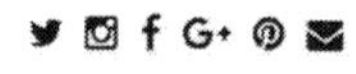

Win £500 to spend at Houseology

December 9, 2015 by **AMANDA COTTINGHAM** **6 COMMENTS**

Well hello lovely readers!

I have a real treat for you today, as I have teamed up again with one of my favourite brands (you may remember from this post) **Houseology** – the gorgeous online design store. Today myself, and three other bloggers are all launching giveaways to win a whopping £500 voucher to spend at Houseology. That's right a whole £2,000 worth of Houseology vouchers in total! Each bloggers voucher can be used on a different category on the site, and mine is side tables!

Mum, wife and writer at The Ana Mum Diary. Lover of all things stylish...read my blog to see interiors, vintage, photography, fashion, beauty, travel and our love for LIFE! I also am the co-founder of the collaborative travel blog below, We Blog Travel... Amanda x

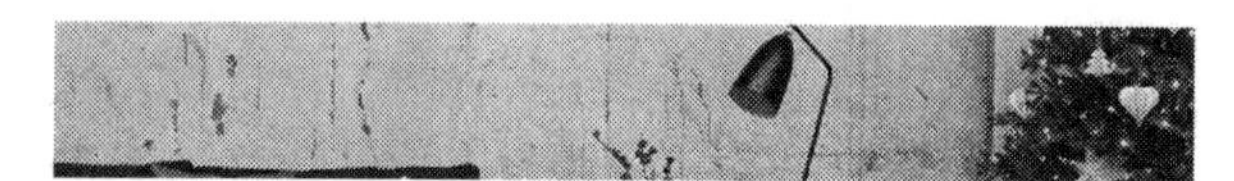

Have A Merry And Bright Houseology Christmas

December 8, 2015

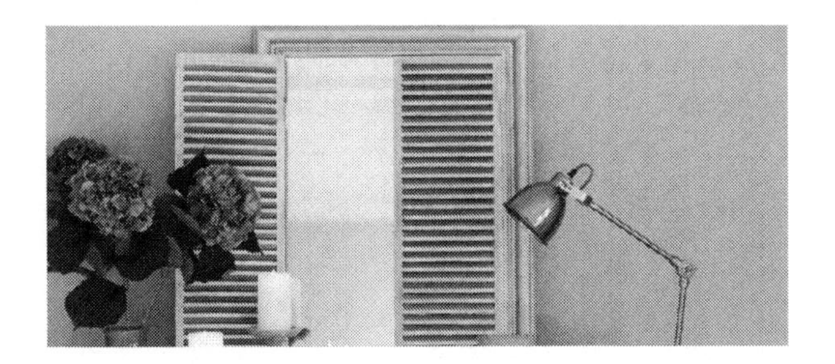

Welcome to The Ordinary Lovely, an award winning family life and interiors blog. I'm Rachel, a sweet toothed, glue gun-wielding mama to two cheeky boys. I like messy beds and old fashioned drinks cabinets.

Top: Muuto Around Ash coffee table Middle: Normann Copenhagen Tablo Tables Bottom: Ercol Originals coffee table

The benefit of running a beast of a giveaway like this is that the company will get a massive boost on social media as a circle of top bloggers are constantly Tweeting updates and sharing the competition, and Houseology's product images, on social media. Those price tags make it too good of an offer not to enter. Not to mention that by running a giveaway with four different bloggers, Houseology are effectively getting four bloggers to vouch for their brand. This builds their brand profile and helps to massively increase brand trust.

Houseology smartly timed this competition to run during the two weeks leading up to Christmas, a time of year when people are much more likely to buy. Giving away a voucher was a great way to get readers onto Houseology's website and browsing their products. You can bet Houseology had a very merry Christmas that year!

Running a mega-giveaway like this is a big task and should only be done if you or someone on your team has experience setting up giveaways and working with bloggers. Many bloggers prefer to work in circles with their own blogger friends and networks, so it's important to bare that in mind if approaching bloggers about a multi-faceted giveaway.

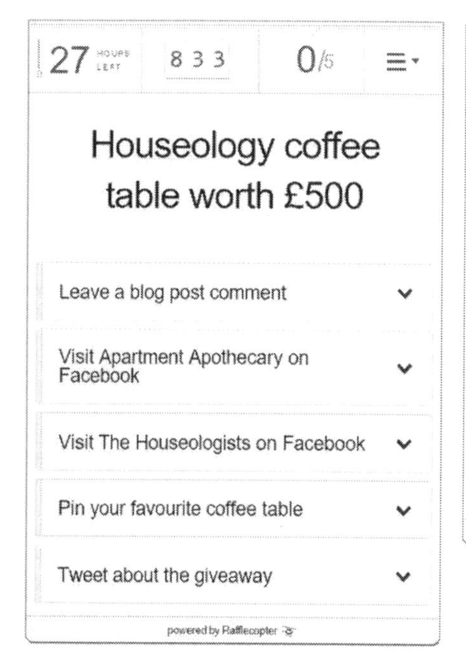

Chapter 11

Blogger Events: Making a Big Impact Outside Your Inbox

We've talked about sponsored content, product reviews and features, running giveaways, and connecting on social media – and they're all key ways to garner some online clout, but what if you really – I mean, *really* – want to get bloggers raving about your brand? In fact, you want those bloggers to love your brand... If you're really determined to get bloggers on board with promoting your business online, then it's time to start thinking outside your inbox and get to know bloggers offline.

In this chapter:

- Know What You Want to Get Out Of It
- Partnering with Other Businesses
- Who's Your Crowd? Choosing Which Bloggers to Invite
- Planning an Absolutely Ninja Blogger Event
- Following Up with Bloggers
- Blogger Event Case Studies

We had an awesome little boutique hotel business in Bath come to us saying they wanted to step up their blogger game. They'd had a couple of bloggers come in for review stays, but the cost of hosting just one blogger each time wasn't working out that well for them financially (because their rooms would usually end up booked on weekends anyway). Still, they loved the gorgeous blog posts and photos taken by bloggers and wanted more of those features – so we put on a blogger event.

The budget was small at just under £400, but that didn't put us off! The hotel would be the event venue, already saving us a significant amount, but in order to make the event as awesome as possible we got on the phone to local businesses and high street brands that the hotel owners loved. High street brand Lush and a local independent chocolatier in Bath agreed to come on board with the event as well. Lush provided complimentary facial treatments and some goodies for the blogger gift bags. The chocolate maker supplied some chocolate tasting boxes for the event itself.

We set a weekend date in late February, which is low season for the hotel, and set a theme we thought bloggers would like. We invited local lifestyle and travel bloggers to the event – especially looking for bloggers who enjoyed producing quirky, boutique style content. In exchange for attending the event, bloggers were asked to credit the hotel, Lush, and the chocolate maker in their blog posts about the event, as well as sending out some social media updates tagging the businesses.

It was a roaring success. The event day was filled with spa treatments, tasty chocolates, champagne, hot tub time, a tour of the hotel, and a talk from the hotel owner about boutique design. Bloggers networked and took a gazillion photos of all the quirkiest elements of the hotel and of all the delicious nibbles on offer. After the event, the blog posts came streaming in, and over 13 blog posts with stylish, targeted content and backlinks went up within 3 weeks.

I don't know about you but these baltic winter months are pretty much my least favourite time of year in the UK. I think they make a convincing case for hibernation! However, if there was anything that was going to get us out the front door in January, it was going to be a spa day in Bath.

Want to know our ninja secrets to organising incredible blogger events without breaking a small business' budget? Of course you do. Here's how we go about it.

Know What You Want to Get Out of It

Blogger events are all about creating a buzz around your brand, but what are your key goals for your event? Do you want to smash it on social? Are you looking for backlinks to gain authority? Do you want to connect with local bloggers and other local businesses? Running a blogger event is one thing, but there's no point running one if you're not reaping the rewards at the end of it. Before you embark on a big event planning mission, write a list of *specific* goals outlining what you want to get out of this event. Leave vague phrases like "lots of exposure" and "some blog posts" out of the equation and get some concrete stuff down (look back at our digital PR goal setting at the beginning of this book for guidelines on writing solid goals). Here are some examples of what your blogger event goals might look like:

Blog Posts and Backlinks from Bloggers

- Gain a blog post including a backlink to our company website from every blogger attending the event, posted within two weeks of the event.
- Get a 2 minute vlog from each of the vloggers to go up on YouTube, uploaded within two weeks of the event.

Social Media

- Have all bloggers Tweeting about the event throughout the day using a brand specific hashtag.
- Involve each blogger in the photo shoot so that they have 8+ gorgeous photos to share on their Instagram feed this season.
- Have goody bag products featured on social media by bloggers and the relevant companies tagged.

Networking with Bloggers

- Network with local bloggers and form relationships in order to partner on brand work in the future.
- Gain insights into specific blogging niches in order to run successful blogger campaigns online.
- Communicate your brand and its USP to bloggers.

In-House Promotional Activity

- Collect amazing photos from the event for social media updates.
- Collect awesome content for a blog post on the company's website.

Social Good

- Raise awareness about a charity or cause.

Partnering with Other Businesses

Many small businesses who are considering running blogger events – and especially those on tight budgets – will often look to partner up with other local businesses. These local businesses will rarely be expected to contribute a budget, however they may offer a venue space, service, products or talk on a specialist topic in exchange for publicity from the bloggers as well.

Partnering with other businesses is a strategy which works very well for local businesses who have friends and connections in the area. Independent business owners are often keen to support one another in raising their profile. Use your contacts and reach out to business owners to see if they want to come on board with your event.

If you are looking for businesses to provide products for goodie bags, you can also send out a request on **Response Source**, an enquiry service which is often used by journalists, bloggers and PR people, to see if there are any businesses who would be interested in sending out sample products in exchange for coverage from bloggers attending your event

Planning an Absolutely Ninja Blogger Event

Running an awesome event takes time, creativity, and drive. If you've got all those things, then even if your budget is tight you can get a great blogger event off the ground and gain exposure for your business and brand. Here are the steps you need to plan a totally ninja event:

1. Time Frames

Make an outline with time frames, a date, and a structure for the event. How long will the event last? Be aware of when bloggers are most likely to be free – many bloggers also have day jobs so won't be available during the Monday - Friday work week. Plan your event at a convenient time, such as the evening after standard working hours or on a weekend if you are requiring bloggers to travel in order to attend. Depending on the style of the event and the location, bloggers may decide to drop-in instead of spending the whole time there, so make this simple and flexible for them.

2. Your Budget

You can't get much done without a little bit of dollar behind you, but you can run a blogger event on just a small budget, especially if you are able to supply the venue yourself. Set a max budget for the event and make a spreadsheet of all the expected expenses, including decoration, equipment, activities, food, and goodie bags.

3. The Location

Where are you going to put all these bloggers? That's a big question – or a small one depending on how many bloggers you're inviting! Having sufficient space is only part of it though; you want a venue that really reflects your brand and the bloggers you invite.

If your business already operates as a venue of some kind, be it a hotel, bar, restaurant, or wedding venue, then your location is already sorted and being on your own turf gives you lots of opportunity for direct brand promotion. If you need to rent a space, go for somewhere that's a blank canvas so that you can put your own stamp on it to represent your brand and your event's theme. You want to have a space that encourages networking and involvement.

4. The Theme

The theme is an important part of making an event enticing for bloggers. You want to select a theme that represents your business and look at a number of variations before deciding on a final theme. The best way to approach the theme is to write down as many relevant themes as you can think of and then narrow it down to the best three.

Let's say you run a traditional wedding dress shop in Cambridge. You're going to be inviting wedding bloggers to your blogger event where you'll be showing off your new dress collection. You partner up with a local wedding venue to host the event. You may choose a theme like "white weddings," "summer weddings," or even "quintessentially British weddings."

Once you've narrowed down your themes to the final three, create a mood board which includes photos and ideas about how each of the event themes would look. Your mood boards can be as creative as you like and should include ideas for activities, decorations, canapes etc. See which theme looks to be the most relevant and appealing but also realistic for your budget.

Here are some of the moodboards our event planning ninjas have made in the past:

Bath Spa Indulgence

Venue Dress
Lighting

Theme

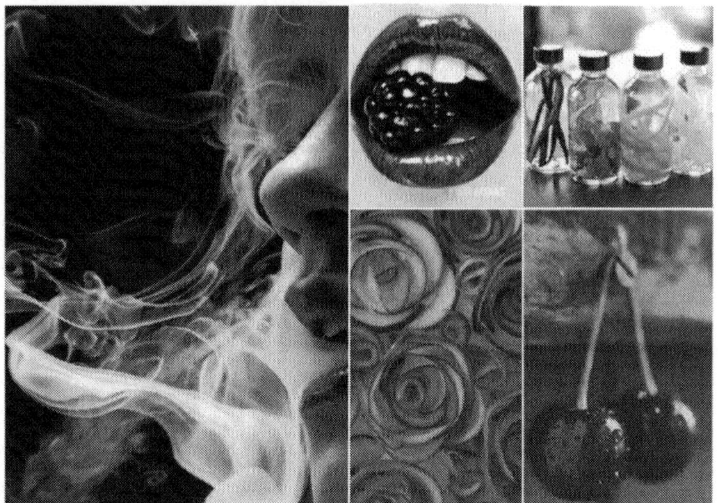

5. The Activities

What's going to happen during your event to give the bloggers some incredible writing and photography material? You don't need to hire someone to put on event activities – instead look at your own skillset and your business' unique selling point. How can you get bloggers engaged with your business and hooked on your USP? There are a whole bunch of different things you can do, but here are some of the most common:

- ***Masterclasses / Workshops / Live Demos***

Masterclasses and workshops are where bloggers learn to do something exciting by getting hands on from the professionals. This could be absolutely anything, be that cocktail making, coffee brewing, knitting socks, practising photography, chocolate making, cooking class, yoga session, silent disco dancing and so on.

- ***VIP Treatments***

Do you run a beauty salon, hairdresser, spa or similar business in the service industry? Offering bloggers a complimentary facial, manicure, hair styling session, massage, or any other spa treatment is the perfect way to get them to blog about exactly what it is you're selling.

- ***Talks***

Give bloggers a story. You want the bloggers to have plenty to write about and giving a talk is the perfect way to communicate this information. Remember that you don't want to just be blurting out facts about your business, but instead package information that's relevant to your business in a way that will spark their interest.

If you own a boutique hotel, talk about what "boutique style" is, where you sourced your boutique style inspiration from and how you got into the boutique hotel market. If you run a community-based tourism tour company, talk about how your travel organisation is making life better for the people in the communities, giving real life examples.

- ***Q&A Sessions***

Following a talk, some of the bloggers may have questions that they would like to ask the speaker. Set aside some time for this so that bloggers will be able to quote you directly on their blog if they have a specific question. This is also a great opportunity for the speaker to promote their company. Record your talks and Q&A sessions so that you can upload them to your YouTube channel as well – it's not only good press for you, but it's also useful for bloggers who may want to reference them.

- ***Interviews***

Some bloggers may prefer to have private interviews with industry specialists and guest speakers. Interviews mean that bloggers are able to create exclusive content for their blog as the answers to their questions haven't been shared publicly with everyone at the event. This is particularly of importance to very niche bloggers who may have more specific questions about your business, work, or the industry in general.

- ***Tours***

If the venue for your event is one which you want bloggers to write about on their blog or showcase on their social media, then give a tour of your venue with plenty of opportunities for bloggers to take photos.

Our boutique hotel would show bloggers around the guestrooms and main spaces, highlighting boutique design elements and discussing art which they are particularly proud of. If the event is based at a wedding venue, take bloggers on a walking tour of the grounds and give them all the information that you would give brides-to-be who are thinking about having their wedding there.

If you run a specialist business where you make your products on-site, such as a craft brewery or a high-end restaurant, give bloggers a "behind the scenes tour" where they can see the masters at work in test kitchens and learn about the development process from start to finish.

6. The Snacks

You can bet that after all these activities (unless you're running a cooking class that is!) everyone will be getting a bit peckish. Some simple canapes and a drink are a fab way to break the ice and get people chatting and networking together. If your food and drink can reflect your event theme, the more so the better. Food ideas may range from more sophisticated restaurant style starters, savoury snacks, or even sushi, to sweet treats, afternoon tea, or decorated cupcakes.

Catering

7. The Goodies

At the end of your event, you don't want bloggers to go home and forget all about it. Pack them off with a goody bag that includes a few product samples, discount vouchers for service based businesses, business cards from all of the companies involved in the event, and a "thank you" card that reminds them that you're looking forward to reading their blog post about the event.

8. The Invites

When the plan is in place, it's time to send some invites. Choosing influencers to invite to your event works in the same way as deciding who to send out products to or host giveaways with, except that location is now an even more important deciding factor. This means looking for bloggers already based in your area or within easy reach of the venue.

Bloggers tend to work in circles with other bloggers in a similar niche to themselves. When you have successfully reached out to a few bloggers, work together with them and invite their friends as well. Look for blogger groups in your local area to see if there are already a group of relevant bloggers who would be keen to attend.

- ***Make a List***

Next, decide how many bloggers your event will be able to accommodate. You can expect some bloggers to turn down the invite, so make a list larger than the initial number of bloggers that you can accommodate.

- ***Connect on Social Media***

As with blogger outreach, you want to connect with your invite list on social media before sending out an official invitation.

- ***Design an Invitation***

When you have set a date and know the outline of the event, it's time to design an invitation. The invitation should be enticing and reflect the theme of your event. Include all relevant details including date, time, and location, as well as the planned activities and the companies who will be involved.

- ***Send Out Invite Emails***

You should send out personalised emails to each blogger. Be sure to state who you are and highlight what they'll get out of the event. Also mention what activities will be happening and what you require from them in exchange. Include an RSVP from **Google calendar** or invite the bloggers to a **Facebook event page** so you can confirm attendees.

- ***Promote the Event***

If you want bloggers to come to you, then it's a good idea to promote your event on your website's blog and social media channels. This can simply be writing a blog post about the upcoming event, creating a Facebook event, and posting some social media updates. You may also decide to promote your event on a blogger network.

9. Follow Up

After the event, send out an email or Tweet to all the bloggers to thank them for coming once again. You will want to stay in touch with the bloggers who you have invited as what they write about your brand is now in their hands. After a week, chase them up by email to ask them how their blog post, photos, social media updates, or any other coverage they've agreed to is coming along. There's no harm in a friendly reminder and many bloggers will happily let you know their progress to date. Be sure to ask the bloggers to email over their links afterwards so that you can share them on your company's social media profiles too.

Blogger Event Case Studies from Big Name Brands

Awesome blogger events come in all different shapes and sizes. While we've mainly focused on how small businesses can use blogger events to harness some blogger power, there's a lot to be learned from household name businesses who have run blogger events. Let's take a look at what they did right and what they didn't:

Case Study #1: Pizza Hut's stuffed crust pizza

In 2013, Pizza Hut released a new 3 cheese stuffed crust pizza. Instead of just running a bunch of expensive TV ads or sending bloggers a voucher for a free pizza, Pizza Hut surprisingly invited bloggers on a "FAM" or familiarisation trip — we usually see travel and tour companies running these kinds of trips to promote locations, but consumer brands have used them effectively in the past as well. Pizza Hut wanted to give bloggers a brand experience and an in-depth insight into how developing a new product works, so they flew them out to Austin Texas, took them on a tour of a Pizza Hut restaurant with their executive chef, took them to a BBQ dinner (huh?), and took them to a party hosted by MTV. Bloggers got to sample the new stuffed crust pizza as well, of course.

This event was both hit and miss. Some of the bloggers loved the whole experience — they were wined and dined and had plenty to write about. Let's face it, there's not all that much to write about if they'd just given the bloggers a free pizza. But was the experience relevant enough to Pizza Hut's brand? Foodbeast publisher Elie Ayrouth didn't think so. She criticised the event for not being "situated in a photo-friendly area" say it'd have been better to be in "a test kitchen or a well-lit room — where tastemakers and influencers can taste the new product, take photos or video, ask questions and interact."

Case Study #2: Laura Ashley's Crafting Afternoon

Home and clothing brand Laura Ashley hosted a craft workshop event in Spring 2015. They invited craft bloggers based in the city for an afternoon of crafting with new floral fabrics and wallpapers from their seasonal range. They partnered up with Crafty Hen, a local craft workshop business in Bristol, who led the event and showed bloggers how to use the materials to design their own DIY notebook covers and fun accessories. At the end of the event, bloggers received a Laura Ashley goody bag to take home. This is an example of a successful local event. Laura Ashley targeted specific niche of craft and design bloggers who were engaged with the event's workshop. The bloggers produced blog posts complete with beautiful photographs of how they'd used Laura Ashley's new fabric ranges and Laura Ashley themselves reciprocated by putting up their own blog post on the event.

Case Study #3: Sisterhood Camp

Sisterhood camp is a bit different from other blogger events, as this one was organised by the bloggers themselves. At the helm is Lou, the blogger behind Little Green Shed Blog. During the summer of 2015, her and a group of bloggers organised a blogger based event in partnership with local businesses in Cornwall. The bloggers stayed at Loveland Farm, a glamping site near Bude. The bloggers received products from local fashion and crafts businesses. These products were used for photography shoots and during craft activities that featured in blog posts after the event. The workshops and activities included tye-dying clothes, learning to make head garlands from wildflowers, and eating a supper prepared by a homemade food events business.

All of these businesses received coverage and links from the 20+ bloggers who attended the event. Because the bloggers organised the event themselves, the businesses had far less to do, but it also meant that the bloggers were really engaged as they had chosen to come together for the event off their own backs.

Chapter 12

On-Site Blogging: How to Create a Killer Blog that Attracts Customers to Your Website and Gets Conversions

Blogs are taking over the internet. Well, that may be a little bit of an exaggeration – more like cat videos and top 10 lists on BuzzFeed are taking over the internet – but it is true that the art of blogging is becoming increasingly appreciated online. Now every savvy business and their competitor has their own business blog because they know that's what they need to climb up those Google rankings. It also helps to get the word out that they know what they're talking about.

In this chapter:

- Why You Need to Start a Blog for Your Business Right Now!
- Get Started with Blogging: 3 Easy Steps to Build Your Blog
- Capture Your Customers: How to Write Blog Content that Will Dramatically Improve Your Sales
- Headache Free Ways to Think Up Blog Topics that Pull in New Customers
- Blogging Questions You Need to Know the Answers To
- Getting the Word Out on the Street: What To Do After Posting a Blog
- Measuring Your Blog's ROI (Yes, it's Worth It)

Big companies like Starbucks and Marks & Spencer don't have blogs on their website just for the fun factor. These are smart businesses know that their on-site blog brings great SEO benefits, provides valuable content for existing customers, gives them content to share on social media, improves their likelihood of reaching new customers, boosts conversions, and can even be an awesome way to generate a buzz about their business online.

> **"60% of businesses that blog acquire more customers"**
>
> Figures from HubSpot survey

Businesses that blog will always be more likely to acquire customers because they're creating content that helps new customers discover the website, get them engaged with the brand and products, and encourage them to come back to the website for more. Well crafted blog content is also a great way of getting potential customers to linger around your website for longer.

Your blog posts are webpages that Google indexes. A blog strengthens your on-site SEO, lets you target specific keywords, and builds internal links to other relevant pages on your website. If you're a lighting company then when Christmas rolls around you'll want to be focusing on shifting as many boxes of fairy lights as possible – or even better selling a huge order to an events company. Some well placed blog posts in the lead up to Christmas on how to decorate your home for Christmas and inspirational images of Christmas themed events with fairy lights could really make for a merry Christmas for your sales.

I know what you're thinking: that all sounds great, but you just don't have the time. You've got countless other things to do to get your business off the ground. You need to focus on the core of your business, there are clients to respond to, orders to process, staff to manage, not to mention the state of your email inbox. Blogging is right at the bottom of your priority list. Am I right, or am I right?

When it comes to investing the time in your business' blog, trust us – it's worth it. Whether it's you writing the blogs, whether your whole team on board with blog writing, or whether you outsource it to a freelance blogger, you want to get that blog pumping out some good content. Create a simple blogging schedule and stick to it. That could just be setting aside two hours every Thursday afternoon to write up a blog post for the following week, assigning a blog writing task to a new team member every Monday, or getting a freelance blogger to write and post a blog every Wednesday.

We've seen countless businesses with deserted blogs on their website because they just don't have time to maintain them. Maybe the last blog post was even from way back in July 2011. Or maybe they've just been using their blog like it's some kind of SEO looting pit and throwing up 200 words of odd text littered with keywords in the hope Google will recognise it. Well, it's 2016 now and Google wants to see you posting a blog every week – and they want it to be decent. It's time to kick the tumbleweed outta' the desert and write some thing that's worth reading.

Easier said than done? I hear you.

You grab a coffee, sit down at your laptop, open up a Word document and – you're dead in your tracks. You'd be surprised how many business owners this happens to. This sudden hot flush of: *What am I going to write about? How am I going to write about it in a witty way? Hell, I'm not witty at all. What if someone reads this and doesn't think what I'm saying is any good? Who even cares about what I have to say anyway?*

If it makes you feel any better, you're not going to be shaking up the universe with your blog – at least not with the first five blog posts. You've got some time to find your own way and settle on a blogging style. Another thing to remember is that everyone else who blogs experiences these exact same feelings – hey, even professional writers experience these kinds of blocks from time to time. But if you've got a product or service that's good enough to sell, then it's damn well good enough to blog about too.

What do you do?

You do it anyway. While your competitors are still working on finding the time and breaking through the fear, you've got the chance to start outpacing them, outranking them, and outselling them by making the decision to go for it. Not everyone is a natural born writer, but you don't need to be to have a good blog. All you need is some useful information to share.

While your expertise might seem like second nature to you, you can bet that other people don't have a clue about these things. Just take a look at the most searched for topics were in 2013 according to **Google Trends**:

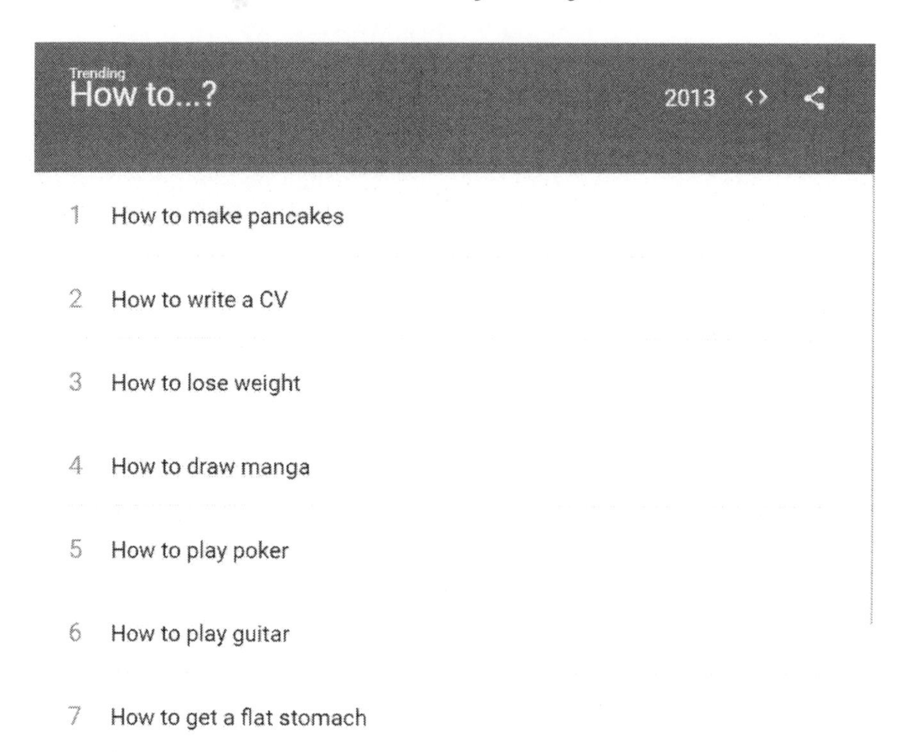

These search terms aren't exactly cryptic questions, but they're things that people just don't know the answer to! There are plenty of small business owners who would be well positioned to answer these queries on their own blogs. You don't have to be an expert chef with your own range of breakfast cookbooks to write a blog post on "how to make pancakes" – if you're an ecommerce website selling spatulas and mixing bowls, you could definitely write a blog post about that topic.

Equally, if you work in the fitness industry as a personal trainer, then there are a number of topics that you could write based on these questions. For #1, a good variation would be "how to make healthy pancakes with just 3 ingredients" or "how to make low fat pancakes." #3 could become a blog post on "how to lose weight without crash dieting" and #4 could become "5 killer exercises to get you the flat stomach you've always dreamed of."

We're getting a bit ahead of ourselves here though. Before you can crack on answering the all the relevant Google search queries on your blog, you need to get your blog set up.

Get Started with Blogging: 3 Easy Steps to Build Your Blog

Before you start blogging, you'll ideally already have a ninja website set up with well optimised webpages that are chock full of well targeted, naturally used keywords telling Google that this is the place to be for information on your business's products or services. You can do even better though. Google's 'bots love fresh content, and a new blog post means that they have a reason to crawl your website again.

A website that doesn't get regularly updated can easily slip down the rankings because Google sees them as stagnant. Don't be that business owner. Start as you mean to go on and keep up the momentum with your blog. You don't have to be an industry giant to do a great job with your blog. Even the little guys can enjoy get good traction and gain conversions from their blogs when done right.

Step 1 — Decide on Your Blog's Focus

"Writing about your company" doesn't count as the answer for this one, so don't even think about it – you're not trying to launch a blog full of redundant press releases to bore everyone's socks off. You want an exciting and enticing blog full headlines that people can't resist clicking on. You want to create a blog that no one ever wants to leave. However, before you can go about doing it, you need to know who those people landing on your blog in the first place are.

Who are your target customers? Where are they from? What age are they? Which gender? What's their job? What do they do in their free time? Aaand – here's a good one – what else do they read? This one is key. You can check out some articles in magazines and blogs related to your business and see what kind of content is popular and what gets the most shares on social media – that's the stuff you want.

Armed with all of that knowledge, you'll be able to hone the focus of your blog's content to make sure that it appeals directly to the people that you're trying to sell to.

Step 2 — Get It Up

The next step is to pick a platform for your blog and get it set up. Don't batten down the hatches just yet! It's more straightforward than you think. You may already have a website with a built-in blog like Wordpress, which is sweet because then the decision is made for you. This is really the best case scenario as it means setting it up will be easy, navigation will be straightforward, and your blog and website will be consistent.

If you're not in the lucky group of website owners who already have a built-in blog then you'll need to grab a seperate blogging platform. We nearly always recommend **Wordpress** because it's the most user-friendly and SEO-friendly. Adjusting the appearance and using plugins to improve functionality can all be done without too much pain. If you're going for Wordpress then you need to choose between hosted and self-hosted. Self-hosted blogs live on your own hosting, whereas hosted blogs live on Wordpress servers. If I were you, I'd go with self-hosted as you have more control over the blog layout, appearance, and domain name. Self-hosted Wordpress is a free download from wordpress.org.

It's really important that your blog is part of your main website and not hosted on an unrelated domain because you want your business's website to reap all of the SEO and traffic related benefits that come with blogging. Definitely grab yourself an SEO plugin – I recommend using **Yoast** – so that you can easily optimise your blog posts with your target keywords. You can add plugins on your Wordpress dashboard. If you're not all that techy, then follow along with some instructions or a tutorial video on how to set up a self-hosted Wordpress blog – there are a number of useful and free guides around. If you get completely stuck, then you can drop an email to support@exposureninja.com and we'll put you in the right direction.

Step 3 - Brand Your Blog

It's sad but true. If your blog doesn't look sexy then people won't be hanging around for too long. You want your blog to be branded just as sexily as your website and your social media channels – and that branding MUST be consistent. If it's not consistent then people won't realise that it's all the same company. Include your company logo, use the same colour scheme, and create consistent imagery.

If you're a dab hand at taking photos or putting together graphics then sweet; you're set. If you're not a professional but you want to give it a go, then there are great programs online, such as **Canva**, where you can create graphics for your website, blog, and social media. If you're design illiterate, then think about outsourcing some of the graphics to a professional designer.

You can find freelancers on websites like **UpWork** and **Fiverr**. You don't have to go OTT with your blog design though. Some businesses keep their blog designs very simple and this works very well.

Check out Rowen & Wren, a UK homewares company, who have a very minimalist, white background blog design:

Don't be afraid to be a bit different with your blog design though, as long as it's in line with your brand. Juniqe, a European poster and arty home accessories e-commerce website, have a very unique and highly visual blog which is designed to look like a magazine with cut outs. This can work really well if your brand is all about visuals.

You won't regret making that initial investment in making your website and blog look absolutely kick-ass. If you don't do it in the beginning, it'll only come round to bite you in the butt later. Look at your blog, compare it to a competitor's blog, and then compare it to an industry giant's blog. You want to be way better than your competitor and standing up as tall as you can against an industry giant.

Headache Free Ways to Think Up Blog Topics that Pull in New Customers

Now that your blog is setup, you need some original and relevant blog topic ideas so that you can start creating killer content. Initially you might have a small flood of ideas of what to write about, but those can soon start to dry up after the first few posts. It's a good idea to plan ahead and come up with a bunch of different blog topic ideas so that you don't lose pace with posting.

Start with Simple Search Techniques

The best way to begin is to think about your target keywords. What search terms do you want to rank for on Google? Your keywords will usually be a good starting point for themes that you can write about on your blog, and writing about topics that relate to these keywords will do wonders for your website's SEO.

Imagine you're a hairdresser. Your salon provides various hairdressing services, such as wash and cuts, hair care, hair styling, bridal hair styling, colouring, perms, and straightening. These services will likely also reflect the hairdresser's target keywords. All of those different services can be used as categories for the blog to split content into different areas. With those categories to hand, it's time to start thinking of blog topics to go under each one. Let's take "hair styling." A quick trick to get started is to open up Google search and type your keyword into the search bar. This will bring up the most searched for terms related to this keyword:

If our hairdresser is mainly a women's hair specialist, then "hairstyles for long hair" could make for a good blog post, but they might decide to cross off "hairstyles for men" as men aren't their target customer. "Hairstyles for long hair" is still a really broad topic though, so refresh Google and type in "hairstyles for long hair" to get some more specific blog topic ideas:

From this list, you can gather that people are most interested in finding out what hairstyles are on trend for 2015 and learning how to do them step by step. Our hairdresser could decide to write a top 10 list of long hairstyles that are on trend in 2015 to get started. She could also create DIY hairstyle tutorials for long hair with step by step photographs of long hairstyles that they have styled in their salon. The latter topic is a really great way to show off your skills to potential customers and get them to trust in your service – making them more likely to book an appointment at your salon. These kinds of photos and tips also make for really strong social media content.

You can repeat this little trick over and over again to come up with blog topics for each of your categories or to go even more in depth and hone in on one very specific and targeted topic.

Answer Common Questions

While Google can show us some of the most common questions that are searched for, you may also receive questions from your customers, or even from friends and family. What are they asking you? These kinds of questions might seem really simple to you – an expert in your industry – but if someone is asking them, then it means they're not the only one who doesn't know.

Let's take a look at our hairdresser again. It's December in the UK now and she has customers coming into her salon with really dry, windswept hair. They sit in the chair, pull at their hair, make a face and ask: "Why does it get so dry? How do I take care of my hair in winter? Should I wear a hat all the time? I don't want to get hat hair." Great, good questions. Let's think about some common questions people might have about haircare:

1. Why is my hair so dry?
2. Why is my hair so frizzy?
3. How can I keep my hair looking healthy and shiny?
4. Does washing my hair too often make it dry?
5. How often should I wash my hair?
6. Do I need conditioning treatment for my hair?
7. What products are best for taking care of my hair?
8. Should I always wear a hat to protect my hair in cold weather?

Thanks to just one question from a customer, our hairdresser has come up with 8 topics she could use to write blog posts. There are two great things about using customer questions: 1) you are directly solving problems for your customers, and 2) your staff should know the answer to these questions as well. Why is the second important? If you don't have time to write up all of these blog posts yourself, you can ask one of your staff to take care of writing it!

Piggyback onto Trending Topics

If you really want to start getting some traction with your blog and reach out to a whole new audience of potential customers – and you want to do it quick! – you're going to want to seek out trending news stories and articles relating to your niche. You can piggyback off the authority of hot topics by writing articles, opinion pieces or responses on your blog and attract readers on social media and through commenting on big news pieces.

How do you find trending topics in your industry? Let's go back to our hairdresser. She's based in the UK, so she wants to look for UK news stories relating to haircuts and hairstyles. She goes to **Google News** to search for the latest news articles and types in something simple like "new haircut." Here are the search results:

Hello! Adele Chopped Her **Hair** Into a Chic Long Bob
GoodHousekeeping.com - 17 hours ago
Over the weekend, everyone's favorite crooner Adele said goodbye to her longer locks and "hello" (hyuck hyuck) to her brand **new** long bob.

Unmasked Derrick Rose Sports **New Haircut** In Chicago ...
Pippen Ain't Easy - 19 hours ago
Chicago Bulls PG Derrick Rose showed up for shootaround on Saturday without his face mask, and he was also sporting a **new haircut**.

Does Kate Middleton's Dicey **Hair** Cut Signal The End of ...
Observer - 12 hours ago
... courtesy of a **new haircut**. Mermaid hair, the center-parted, long bent sided look made famous by the Kardo-Jenners was chopped for good.
Kate Middleton: Hairdresser Reveals Why Busy Mom Chopped Her ...
Hollywood Life - 11 hours ago
Explore in depth (169 more articles)

Emma Watson Just Unveiled A Chic **New Haircut**
TeenVogue.com - 8 Dec 2015
Emma Watson's **hair** has gone through many evolutions — there was the frizzy pouf of Hermione Granger (a style that Emma admits still makes ...
Emma Watson's **New Haircut** Proves She Can Pull Off Just About ...
Huffington Post - 9 Dec 2015

On just the first page of results, there are three very popular celebrities who have had new haircuts that everyone is talking about right now. There's also an article relating to a sportsman in Chicago, which our hairdresser can immediately cross off as she's based in the UK. Out of the three celebrities on the list, our hairdresser thinks that Kate Middleton's new hair cut is the most interesting and relevant to her target customer. So she decides to write an article giving her expert opinion on how the new haircut looks on Kate, what it's going to mean for hairstyle trends in 2015, and which face shapes can pull off this kind of chop.

Depending on your business, it might be the case that there's just not that much going on in the mainstream news to get excited about. If our hairdresser decided that celebrity hair wouldn't be a great blog topic for her particular salon, or that when she was searching there weren't any particularly relevant or newsworthy stories, then she might want to look at what content is getting people excited and is being shared on the internet.

Buzzsumo is a really fun online software that looks at what content is most popular on the internet at that time for any given website or search term. It will also show you the number of times the article has been shared on social media. You can use a very basic version of Buzzsumo for free to get started with. Just head to the homepage and use the search bar:

Our hairdresser types in the same search term that she used when looking for news stories on Google, and here are the results:

Wow! Look at those share figures on the right. Looking down the list, our hairdresser reckons that "short hairstyles" is a bit of an overdone topic, crosses off the "billionaire barber" as being an irrelevant story, and decides that the topic that most stands out to our hairdresser is the "pixelated hair technique" which got 145k shares on Facebook. She clicks through to the article, grabs some inspiration from these crazy hair colouring techniques and decides to get an article up on her blog about these cutting edge hair designs.

Jorge Cancer, a press rep for X-Presion, told Bored Panda that the style "*was created by mistake. We were in Minneapolis preparing a big show for 4500 people and then, with one of the models, I got an effect in her hair that I didn't expect. After that, we started to study and think until we got the trend as it is now*" (Image credits: laialae)

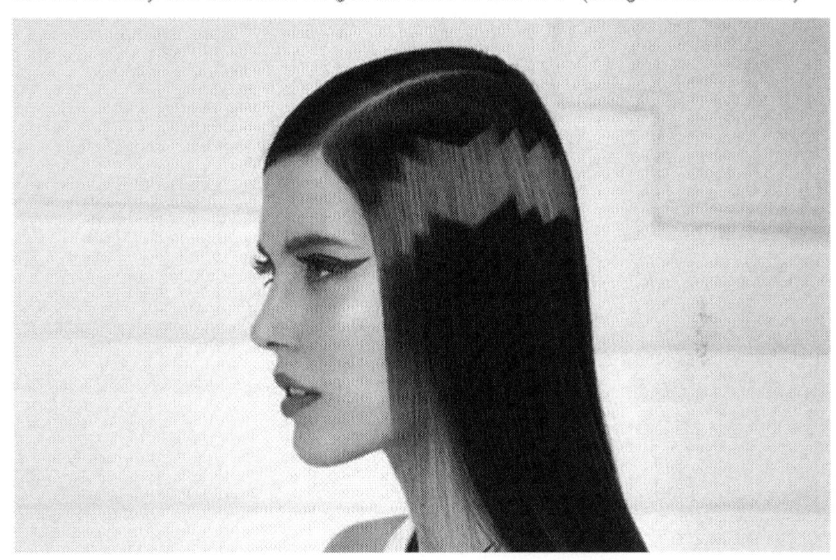

You can do the same for just about any industry or niche. Remember though, you don't just want to regurgitate content that's already been written elsewhere. Readers will go straight to the Guardian, the Huffington Post, Forbes, or some other big news outlet for that. What you want to do is add something valuable to the discussion – you might have a controversial opinion, maybe you agree with one side of the argument, perhaps you would have handled this news differently, or maybe you even have relevant case studies to include.

Tip! Don't Just Blog about Your Business

When you start writing, you might be immediately tempted to try and write content that sticks rigidly to your products or services. It's awesome to mention your products and/or services where relevant but you don't want to bombard your readers with a bunch of overly promotional writing packed with product recommendations – because that's a complete turn off, they won't read it and it doesn't look professional.

It's okay to branch out a little with your blog post content. Think about your blog like an umbrella that can cover a variety of topics within your niche. A great example of a business blog that does a spectacular job of this is eco-conscious bamboo clothing brand, *Braintree*. Their blog, which is called *Bthoughtful*, covers clothing but branches out to include DIY projects using eco-friendly materials and home cooked recipes for seasonal, locally sourced ingredients.

The idea here is to create a blog with content that their audience with love – and that means extending beyond the realms of bamboo clothing. They know that their readers are eco-aware, are interested in eco-friendly DIY projects and ideas, and care about their homes.

The golden rule about blogging is that it's not about you, it's about your audience.

Capture Your Customers: How to Write Blog Content that Will Dramatically Improve Your Sales

Deciding on a blog topic is only half the battle. The other half comes when you actually have to write the blog. While you could just put your fingers to the touchpad and smash out 600 words on your chosen topic, you'll just end up with a block of text that is too off-putting for anyone to read to the end. There are a couple of points that you need to consider if you really want to grab your reader's attention and convert them into customers – and if you're struggling to start writing then planning these things out first will give you a good article skeleton.

Don't write boring headlines.

Oh my god, please do not title your blog post "Top 10 Things To Do in London" – I think I've read that a bazillion times before and I'm starting to not give two red buses.

Here's a stat for you: on average, 8 out of 10 people will read a headline, but only 2 out of 10 will actually read the rest of the article. That's huge.

It just goes to show how critical a killer headline is. To beat that average, you need headlines that are striking and so irresistible that a potential reader can't help but click on them to find out more. There are lots of popular types of headlines out there. After analysing nearly a million headlines, the guys at OK Dork found out that the most shared headlines are as follows:

Most Popular Words/Phrases
In Highly-Shared Headlines

Word/Phrase	# of uses	% of headlines
List Post	787	11.10%
You/Your	478	6.74%
Free/Giveaway	255	3.60%
How To	205	2.89%
DIY	197	2.78%
I/Me/My	153	2.16%
Easy	137	1.93%
Win	104	1.47%
New	97	1.37%
Ways	75	1.06%
Why	60	0.85%
Video	51	0.72%
The Most	17	0.24%

- List posts
- You/Yours
- Free/Giveaway
- How To
- DIY

Just because list posts comes in at number one, this isn't to say that you should start churning out "Top 10s" all over the place. But when you're deciding what headline to put on your blog post, you definitely want to take note of the headlines that get the most clicks and shares and vary between these different types to attract the most readers you can.

Say we're a fitness instructor this time. Our fitness instructor has checked out some frequently searched for topics and decided to write a blog post on "how to lose weight." He's not just going to title the blog "How to Lose

Weight" – because that's too plain. He thought about titling it "Top 10 Ways to Lose Weight" – but decided that sounded a bit middle of the road. Let's plug the topic into some of the popular headline styles from above and see what we get:

1. 7 Ways to Lose Weight
2. Ways YOU Can Lose Weight
3. How You Can Lose Weight
4. An Ultimate Guide to Losing Weight

All of these sounds pretty good. We already know that #1, the list post, is probably going to get the most shares out of those titles, but if our fitness instructor was planning on writing a longer blog post covering more aspects of weight loss, they might decide to go for #4 instead. We can probably go one step better than this though. If we check out what's topping the most popular lists on the big content sharing websites like BuzzFeed and Bored Panda right now, here's what we get:

1. 18 Posts That Prove Coconut Oil Is The Solution To All Of Life's Problems
2. Here's The Answer To Everyone's Biggest Question About "Love Actually"
3. 24 Dump Dinners You Can Make In A Crock Pot
4. 15 Cheesy One-Pot Pastas That'll Nourish Your Soul
5. Here's What No One Tells You About Having Both Depression And Anxiety
6. The Truth Behind Online Photos Revealed In An Eye-Opening Video
7. 18 Hybrid Animals That Are Hard To Believe Actually Exist
8. Donkey Smiles From Ear To Ear After Being Rescued From Flood In Ireland

Looking at these we can decipher some definite trends here. Many of these blog posts are going to solve a problem or answer a question that we had: "The Solution To All Of Life's Problems" and "Here's The Answer To." Many evoke emotions: "That'll Nourish Your Soul" (healthiness, happiness), "Having Both Depression And Anxiety" (sadness), "The Truth Behind" (curiosity, surprise). Some are just plain kooky: "18 Hybrid Animals," and "Donkey Smiles From Ear To Ear".

Sure, a lot of these titles are quite sensationalist, but that's all part of standing out among a sea of other headlines. It's fair enough if you don't want your blog to read like the home page of BuzzFeed (and probably a good thing), but you can still use a lot of these same ideas to entice readers – make their life easier, answer their burning questions, spark their emotions, or give them something totally unexpected.

A Foolproof Headline Formula

For businesses, we've found that there's one particular headline formula that always grabs attention – offers without potential objection. Yes, you got it. Your customer wants something awesome and they don't want to sacrifice anything in order to get it! Here's how the formula works:

Offer + Time + Without Potential Objection

Our personal trainer plugs his weight loss topic into the formula and now he has:

- Lose Weight in 30 Days Without Dieting

A beauty school running hairdressing courses could use this formula for a blog like:

- Learn to Create Perfect Bridal Hairstyles in Just 5 Days that Can't Go Wrong

Anyone interested in losing weight or learning new bridal hairstyles couldn't possibly not click on that title to find out more.

Other Effective Headline Formulas

If you want to mix it up a bit, then try experimenting with a couple of different headline formulas. Everyone's customers are different, so what gets incredible results for one business won't necessarily work for another. Don't be afraid to experiment – see what kinds of headlines are most popular among your readers. Here are a couple of other headline formulas that we love:

Trigger word + Adjective + Keyword + Promise

Example: How You Can Become a Ninja Writer in Less than 24 Hours

Number + Adjective + Keyword

Example: 12 Meticulous Habits You Need to Become a Writing Ninja

A Quick Way to [solve a problem]

Example: A Quick Way to Beat Your Competitors on Google

Use Headings and Bullet Points

Internet users have a short attention span. The average blog reader will only last for 15 seconds or less before they bounce off to another blog. By making a blog post less like a big block of text and more like manageable, bite-sized chunks, you can keep readers on the page for longer. The best way to do this is to use relatively short paragraphs, break up the text with headings throughout, and use bullet point lists where appropriate. These allow readers to skim the content and get the jist of what's going on if they don't have enough time to read the post in full, and for you to communicate key information by making it stand out.

I mean, come on, would you rather read this?

ranking, all on your own terms. Yet so few businesses maintain an active blog, typically either treating it as a place to dump SEO content or trying to ignore the fact that their well-intentioned weekly posting schedule got forgotten after three weeks... two years ago. The hardest part of blogging is starting, and the second hardest part is keeping it going. There always seems to be better things to do, and besides — what could we possibly write about anyway? Who would be interested in what *we* have to say? These thoughts seep and put an end to most blogs even before the first key is pressed. I've spoken to countless confident business owners and leaders in their fields who talk about being unable overcome the fear that their blog will be judged by peers, customers and the wider world. What if the audience doesn't like what they say? What if they make a mistake and look stupid? What if their authority crumbles around them as their blog reveals for the first time that the emperor is, in fact, wearing no clothes? These fears are far from unusual, and almost everyone new to blogging faces them at some point. The first truth is that any blog is unlikely to get this amount of attention in the early days. Unless you are already extremely high profile, your blog is unlikely to make a significant dent in the universe for the first 5 posts, so you have a bit of time to find your feet. The second truth is that these worries are exactly the same worries that everyone else shares. Almost everyone who decided to build their own profile faced the same worries when they started. The difference between the winner and the loser is deciding to go for it anyway, whilst competitors remain paralysed by the fear of their blog becoming fantastically popular.

Or this?

10. Embrace Social Media

Social Media sites such as **Facebook** and **Twitter** are possibly the most important part of building your travel blog and it's brand. It's where a lot of your potential future traffic is going to come from, so it's **essential** that people are easily able to find even if they're not on your website.

For instance, here at **TravelDoIt** we have our Twitter account name which is @traveldoit and we also have the Facebook page facebook.com/traveldoit which makes it extremely easy for people to find us.

What you need to do is to check that your potential account name is free on these social media platforms and any other useful websites such as Tumblr and **Pinterest**, and the best way to do this is by using a service like Namechk.com

So what's left to do?

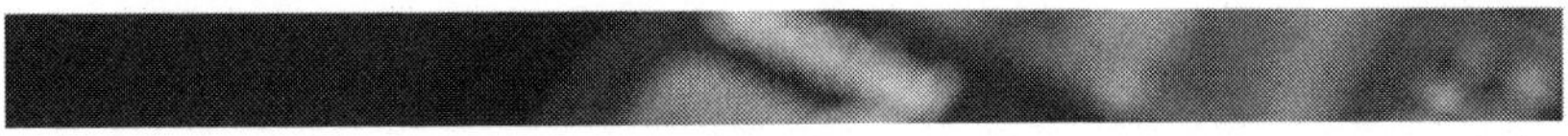

(via traveldo.it)

Don't write text dumps, okay.

Use Visual Content & Embedded Media

Humans are visual creatures: we all love incredible photos, cool infographics, and interesting videos. Embedding rich media into your blog is a sure fire way to keep your readers on the page for longer. When it comes to photos, personal ones of real life projects and people are more appealing than generic stock photos as they build brand trust. However, if you don't have access to any relevant, personal images, then stock photos can definitely get the job done.

Stock Images vs Your Own Images

Ideally, you'll have some of your own photos of the work you do in your business, of your employees, and so on. The problem with stock photos is that they're just that, the same old stock that everyone has seen before. While stock photos might look "perfect", they can come across as sterile. People love to see *real* photos, they feel that they're more authentic and authenticity is better every time. Potential customers will trust your brand more if the photos on your website are actually of *your* employees and *your* services/products in action.

Have you seen this woman before, or one just like her?

Sure you have. She's the stock image for the customer service team on hundreds of websites. People know that she's not going to be the person they're actually talking to when they ring up your customer service team. She's a model, she doesn't work in a call centre, they know it, and it impacts their decisions. Try to use images of your own staff where possible and establish that personal connection with potential customers. It doesn't matter if your photography isn't perfect or if there are a few awkward smiles in there – that's the human connection you're going for. It makes people feel more comfortable and more trusting towards you and your brand.

Where to Get Stock Photos for Free

We get that it's not always possible to have your own photos for everything. If you're a small business selling living room lamps and you're blogging about home decor and how to style your living room then sure, you're not going to have a showroom and lots of different shots of living rooms to use. But hey, don't go stealing any images straight off of Google. There's a common misconception that you can just Google image search something and use any photo that you want from the search results. But you can't; *that's image theft*.

Images on the internet are not a free for all. When someone uploads a photo to the internet, they retain the copyright to that image irrelevant of whether it is watermarked or not. It means that using those images without permission, even if you credit the source, is illegal. It's true – a whole heap of image theft goes on all over the internet, and the vast majority of it goes undetected. **However**, you do sometimes hear horror stories of people who have been caught out using – sometimes even accidentally – images that they do not have the rights to use and have had to pay out thousands of pounds.

Fortunately, there are a couple of websites where you can get images to use for free. On **Flickr** you're able to use the advanced search function to find images that are under the Creative Commons license. Accreditation may be required on Flickr images. Other free to use image websites that do not require you to credit the photographer or source include **unsplash.com** and **stocksnap.io**. However, it can sometimes be harder to find the images you want on the free sites and you may have to look at paid stock photos instead. There are also plenty of websites where you can buy stock images, such as **Shutterstock** and **Pixabay**.

Infographics

An e-cigarette e-commerce website who we write blog posts for designed some slick looking infographics with useful information about travelling with your e-cigarette, which they also branded with their logo. The infographics were included in a blog post on the website along with an embed code which can be copy and pasted by readers onto their own blogs. The embed code includes a link back to the original blog post, and is a great way to encourage more links to your website and recognition of your brand. If you want to try your hand at designing your own infographics then there are some great websites out there where you can use pre-made templates and plug in your own info and images. **Piktochart** and **Canva** are two of the best for designing infographics. If you don't have an eye for design, then outsource your infographics and other images to a graphic designer to make sure they look pro.

Calls To Action

For the troops who have made it to the end of the blog post, you need one final command before you can fly the flag of victory. Make your readers an offer they can't refuse. One that gets them to buy now because *damn* that's such a good deal or perhaps an offer that will bring them back at a later date – 25% off if they buy a product within the next hour, free delivery on all items, a free download, a free e-book, an opportunity to book a free demo or taster session, or an opportunity to sign up for a newsletter where they can get money off of their first purchase.

Don't use ugly CTAs. Things like "CLICK HERE TO BUY STRAWBERRY FLAVOUR CARTRIDGES" are not going to get people clicking or buying. They look awful and they sound awful. Encourage people to do what you want in an attractive way. That might mean using a lead generation magnet image, a well-worded phrase, or a nice looking widget. Even if your blog doesn't immediately convert a reader into a paying customer, they can still be good leads. A newsletter appearing in their email inbox a week later, a voucher for a free taster session that they have downloaded, or a similar kind of enticing offer means that they are more likely to remember your brand and return to the website again in the future.

One of our clients, an HR software company, have created a 10 week online course which blog readers can sign up to. They don't get the course all in one go – they receive ten weekly installments straight to their inbox via an email newsletter. This technique means that the reader is reminded about the company every week for an extended period of time. They are encouraged to return to the website every week because they are gaining "exclusive" access to valuable information not otherwise available on the website.

SEO Optimising Your Blog Content

Yeah, you got it – just like your website content, you need to make sure that your blog posts are SEO-friendly so that Google's 'bots will like them. Don't panic. We take an in-depth look at SEO in our #1 best selling SEO title: How To Get To The Top Of Google – but let's take a look at the quick ninja things you can do to SEO up your blogs.

Keywords are the words and phrases your audience uses to search for your product or service. For example, if you're a dentist based in Glasgow and your most popular treatment is "six month smile braces" then you might use that phrase in a blog post on "How Six Month Smile Braces Work." This post could include what happens in the treatment, how long it takes, how much it costs, and why your dental practice in Glasgow is the best place to have it done. The words "six month smile braces," and related phrases like "cosmetic braces" and "teeth straightening" would be included in the article so that Google and other search engines are crystal clear that this blog post is about six month smile braces.

Use specific keywords: Ideally, you want to focus on very specific keywords. The more targeted your keywords, the more likely you are to rank well for them on search engines. If our dentist could include "six month smile braces in Glasgow" then that's even better.

Use keywords in your blog title and headings: Keywords should be included in your blog's title and headings throughout the blog post, as well as in the body of the blog. Including keywords in your title is a really important aspect of SEO that will help boost rankings and show your audience exactly what your blog post it all about.

Don't cram in keywords like crazy: You want to use the right density of keywords. Don't just go stuffing in keywords where they don't fit. In the old days, that might've helped but now that semantic search is on the rise you don't need to do that, and Google might even start to think you're being a bit spammy. Write naturally and use keywords naturally.

Use keyword variations (in moderation): Say your target keyword is "dental implants". Ideally, you're going to use those exact words in your article title, subheadings, and a couple of times in the body of your text. But you should use some variations (often naturally occurring) in your writing – for example, we might say "implant dentistry" or even just "implants".

Write a relevant headline: Writing a jazzy article headline isn't all about trying to be the next article that gets featured on Buzzfeed (not that that's a bad goal). It's about writing a title that actually tells the reader what your article is going to be about and tells Google too – by using your keywords. Say our keywords are "boutique hotel Bath". Instead of writing a title like "Where You Should Stay in Bath", a better and more SEO-friendly option would be "10 Boutique Hotels in Bath that All Travellers Will Love" or even something like "Boutique Hotels in Bath – and a Sneak Peek at Their Boutique Design".

Use subheadings: We have subheadings because a) they make articles easier to read, and b) they're suuuper SEO-friendly. Make subheadings descriptive and include keywords when relevant.

Say you're writing an article about the 10 best teeth brushing techniques for kids.

- Example of a bad subheading: 1) Sing Songs
- Example of a great subheading: Teeth-Brushing Technique #1: Sing Songs
- Another good variation: Sing Songs While Brushing Your Kid's Teeth

Include internal links: Using internal links means linking to other pages on your website within your blog post. When someone is reading your blog post, your aim is to turn them into a customer, which means that you need to get them clicking around your website and looking at your stuff. The best way to do this is to link to relevant pages for products, services, related blog posts, and so on. This will reduce your bounce rate (i.e. people will stay on your website for longer, rather than bouncing off after having quick read and getting the info they wanted).

Check out the first paragraph of this blog from Lush's blog, it's got product links in there straight away:

WELCOME TO OUR FRESH HANDMADE BLOG

Dec 12.1

Winter is coming: is your body ready?

Posted In: Product Use >> Tips and Tricks

Every season brings something new: spring has budding blossoms, summer has busy beaches, fall has crisp, colorful leaves, and winter has...dry, itchy skin. Sure, there's plenty to love about winter (who doesn't like **vegan eggnog** and **building a snowman?**), but the effect cold air can have on our skin can put a damper on wintertime fun.

Thankfully, there are ways to protect your skin's delicate moisture balance when the weather starts to get chilly. Check out our suggestions below for keeping your whole body soft and smooth all winter long!

Looking for tips to protect delicate facial skin? Check out our post **Winter is coming: is your skin ready?**

Include external links (to quality websites!): Your blog post is a valuable resource – at least, it should be – and all good resources link to their sources. If you're quoting a research paper, link to it. Quoting a BBC News article? Link to it. Referencing an awesome blogger? Link to them. Linking to your sources shows that you're using credible information and, hey, the internet is all about linking to other webpages and sharing content. Don't link to spammy websites or rubbish resources. If you've lifted a figure or quote from an untrustworthy-looking website that you wouldn't want to link to, then think about whether you really want to be using that info in your awesome blog post.

By the way, **you don't want to link to any of your competitors!** To be safe, simply don't link to anywhere that aims to make money. So if you are writing about dentistry, linking to the NHS website is good, linking to Colgate is iffy, and linking to a different dental practice is unacceptable.

What About Local SEO?

Many small businesses are also local businesses and are trying to reach customers in a certain location rather than nationally or internationally. For example, imagine we're a dentist based in Glasgow and our main target keywords are "cosmetic dentist Glasgow" and "dental implants Glasgow". How can we reach the people of Glasgow and get them to come to our dental surgery? First, we want to mention in our blog posts that we're located in Glasgow. Don't be trying to just smush this into titles and any old place in the article though – we want it to read naturally! Here's what we're going to do instead:

A) Look for article topics related to Glasgow – then we'll naturally want to use that keyword in our writing.
B) If there's not anything too interesting going on in Glasgow, then we'll want to target the keywords of "cosmetic dentistry" and/or "dental implants" with our blog topic. Then, we can include the location of Glasgow in our subheading at the beginning of the article and in our call to action at the end of the article.

SEO Behind the Scenes

Good SEO isn't all about the words you see on the page. There's a lot going on behind the scenes here too that needs to be optimised for SEO as well.

An SEO plugin for Wordpress such as **Yoast** or **All-In-One SEO** can help with this.

SEO optimise images: Google and other search engines can't read pictures alone, which means you need to add text descriptions to say what's in the picture – these are known as alt tags. You should include your keywords in alt tags when possible. In Wordpress you can add alt tags to your images when you upload them and "add media" to your blog post.

Use meta descriptions: Meta descriptions are the preview text description of your post that's shown on Google and social media. A good meta description contains up to 160 characters and catchy enough to make people click.

In the screenshot below you'll see the SEO settings screen of the Wordpress SEO by Yoast plugin. This screen shows the general title and meta description, which are the ones used by Google:

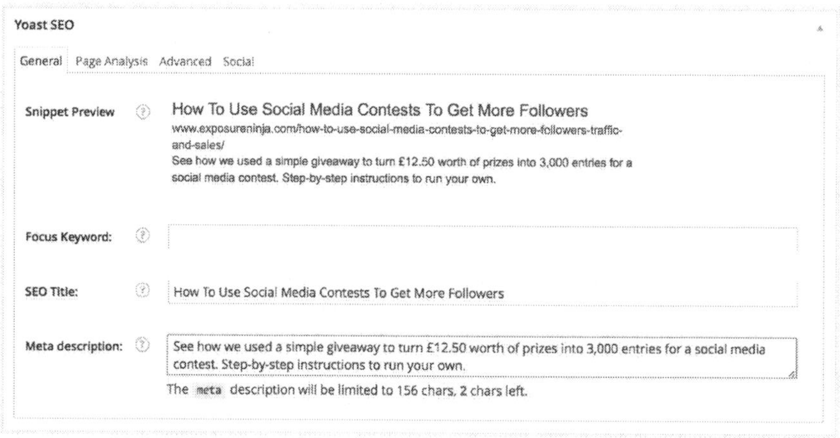

Yoast SEO

General Page Analysis Advanced Social

Snippet Preview: How To Use Social Media Contests To Get More Followers
www.exposureninja.com/how-to-use-social-media-contests-to-get-more-followers-traffic-and-sales/
See how we used a simple giveaway to turn £12.50 worth of prizes into 3,000 entries for a social media contest. Step-by-step instructions to run your own.

Focus Keyword:

SEO Title: How To Use Social Media Contests To Get More Followers

Meta description: See how we used a simple giveaway to turn £12.50 worth of prizes into 3,000 entries for a social media contest. Step-by-step instructions to run your own.
The meta description will be limited to 156 chars, 2 chars left.

You'll notice that there is a tab marked "Social" along the top. This allows you to set separate titles, descriptions, and images to show up when the article is shared on Facebook and Twitter. The description you use for Facebook can be slightly longer (we recommend 200 characters, although Facebook will show up to 300). Twitter's description is limited to 200 characters.

When choosing a photo to show with your blog posts on Facebook or Twitter, use a 1024 x 512 image which is a good ratio for both networks. Keep in mind that any text used in the image needs to be in the centre to avoid it being cropped off.

Optimised the webpage URL: The webpage URL itself should be shortened and target the main keywords of the article – sometimes the title, sometimes just the keywords, sometimes including a category from the blog etc.

Blogging Questions You Need to Know the Answers To

How long should blog posts be?

Blog posts should be an absolute minimum of 300 words. If blog posts are less than 300 words, then that's barely any text or information for Google and other search engines to read. If you're a new blogger then readers may also be put off by the lack of content. Unless you're a guy like Seth Godin – he writes ridiculously short posts – and you're well known enough to have an audience who dig short posts, it's probably not for you.

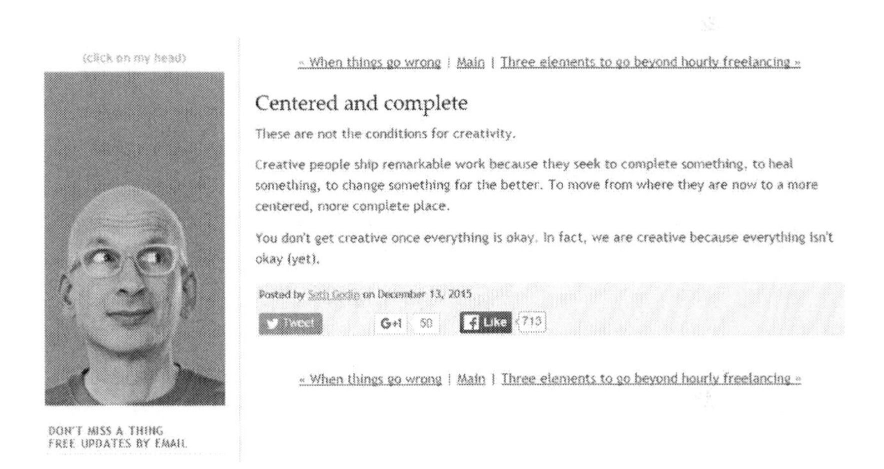

Mid-length blog posts of around 600-800 words are probably your golden ticket. That's a good amount of words to cover some really valuable stuff. It's enough words to get your readers interested without dragging on forever, and they're more likely to finish reading the whole blog post. What's more, 800 words shouldn't take you forever to write.

There is a case for long form blog posts of 1000 words or more as well. More words on the page means search engines are better able to rank posts because there's more text for them to crawl, and blog posts with more words are said to rank higher. However, you do risk your audience finding the content long winded, so long-form blog posts should only be used if you genuinely have a lot of valuable information to share on that one topic.

At Exposure Ninja, we like to mix it up. The average length of our blog post is around 1000 words along with a whole heap of visual media like images and videos to illustrate what we're talking about. But we sometimes do short and sweet 500 word posts and you might even see the odd 1500+ post if we've really got something to write home about! We always recommend varying the length of your blog posts depending on the topic and how in-depth you need to go.

How often should you blog?

Don't be that dried up prune blog that we talked about earlier. There are no set in stone rules about how often you should be updating your blog, but the more you update the better. We recommend that most businesses try to update their blog **at least once a week and at the same time each week** at a bare minimum. If that sounds like an impossible target then it's probably time to spread the load with your staff or consider hiring someone to give you a hand with your blog.

Ideally, you would be posting blogs 2–3 times per week. This gives you enough time to select topics that your audience finds valuable and to share the content that you have already posted on to your blog without oversaturating your readers. If your business is in a fast-paced and cutting edge industry, then you might want to consider posting every day to keep up with the latest trends. For most businesses, posting every day would be beyond the realm of possibility and would be an unnecessary stretch.

Should I respond to reader comments on my blog?

Yes, yes and yes.

In most cases, business owners will choose to allow readers to post comments on their blog posts and this is a great way to interact with potential customers (in a non-promotional way!) Remember that you're more likely to deter people from buying if you're overtly sales focused, and more likely to increase your sales by contributing to a discussion. It shows that you're both friendly and knowledgeable.

It's important to engage with your readers, regardless of whether they're posting positive or negative comments. Hopefully, they'll just be commending you on your awesome blog post – to which you can just say "thanks!" More often, they might have a question to ask relating to your blog post or seek your opinion on something more specific – this is great because it means your audience are really getting involved, they care about what you're saying enough to seek advice, and building loyalty in this way is more likely to get you conversions.

If you're getting a couple of negative comments, then have a discussion with them. Did they raise any valid points? If not, explain your reasoning more clearly. Show that you're fair and easy to talk to and other customers will love that. If you're getting trolls – everyone does at some stage – then throw those comments in the trash. You only want to engage with genuine readers.

Examples of Perfect SEO-Friendly Articles

It's all well and good explaining all this SEO stuff and what a great article looks like, but you want to see the goods right? How does it actually look in practice? Let's Google the phrase "best teas for weight loss". Sounds like a pretty popular topic, something that a decent amount of people will be Googling and with keywords that a lot of businesses will want to be targeting.

Top organic result for the search is eatthis.com/5-best-teas-weight-loss

The article is around 730 words – so it's decently long but not super long. I hit F3 and search the whole keyword phrase – "best teas for weight loss" – which appears twice on the page. (Go on! Go and do it too. See for yourself!)

Not that much, right? But, let's break it down. Within this keyword phrase we also have here two other phrases people will Google a lot – the "teas" and "weight loss." You can bet a pretty penny they appear way more in this article:

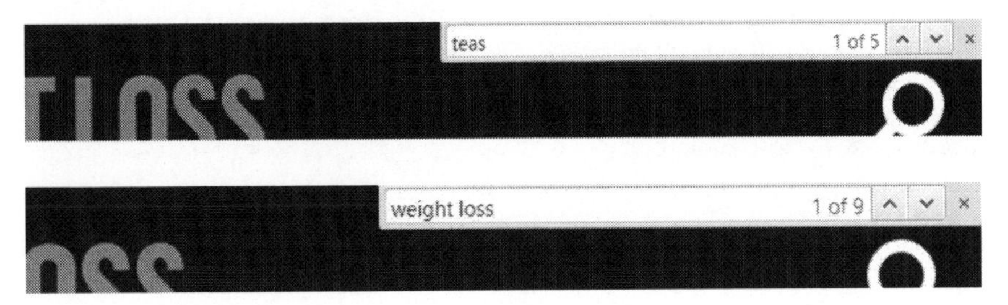

Yep. You can scroll through on F3 and check where in the article those keywords are; for example, here's the first mention of "weight loss" after the article title:

A steaming cup of tea is the perfect drink for soothing a sore throat, warming up on a cold winter's night, or binge-watching *Downton Abbey*. But certain teas are also perfect for doing something else—helping you lose extra weight.

Each of these 5 Best Teas for Weight Loss has its own individual, magic properties, from dimming your hunger hormones to upping your calorie burn to —literally—melting the fat that's stored in your fat cells. Oh, and they can also help reduce your risk of heart disease and diabetes, too. (Stick to 3-4 cups—or

It's right in the introduction there. The more astute with have also noticed that within this introduction we also have keyword variations like "lose extra weight" and a bunch of language around the theme of weight loss – binge, hunger hormones, calories burn, melting the fat, fat cells... Break it down even further and the article includes a whole bunch of different kinds of tea – red tea, white tea, rooibos tea, green tea, oolong tea – and information on how they aid weight loss. Then it links to other tea and weight loss related article on the website (inbound links):

4. THE POUND-A-WEEK MELTER

Oolong Tea

DRINK THIS: Bigelow, Stash

BECAUSE IT: Boosts metabolism

Oolong, a Chinese name for "black dragon," is a light, floral tea that, like green tea, is also packed with catechins, which help to promote weight loss by boosting your body's ability to metabolise lipids (fat). A study in the *Chinese Journal of Integrative Medicine* found that participants who regularly sipped oolong tea lost six pounds over the course of the six-week time period. That's a pound a week! Shed more belly flab—rapidly—with one of the 4 Teas That Melt Fat!

This website is basically creating a massive resource for teas and weight loss – a definitive guide to this topic. In fact, the second organic search result for "best teas for weight loss" is from the same website (!): eatthis.com/21-best-teas-for-weight-loss

Getting the Word Out on the Street: What To Do After Posting a Blog

Coming up with ideas, crafting a killer headline, writing well-structured content, formatting your post, inserting visuals and SEO optimising your blog post is the hard part. It's not over once you've hit publish though. Now that your blog post is up and live, you've got to do a little bit of work to get people coming on over to have a look.

Sharing on Social Media

If you're using Wordpress then you might have realised that you can link up your social media platforms so that they're automatically shared when your blog post publishes. Well, that's cool, but it's not enough. Take a little time to rewrite an update for each of your social media channels, paying attention to what style of content performs best on each channel.

- On **Twitter** you only have 140 characters, so use them wisely. Use 2-3 relevant hashtags and attach a photo to increase engagement.
- On **Facebook** you have more room to write a description, include the blog preview, and include an image. You may want to ask a question at the end to get some responses from your followers. Hashtags aren't very effective on Facebook so leave those out.
- Like Facebook, you can add a more lengthy description on **Google+**, though it's unlikely that you will get a huge amount of, if any, engagement on this channel. Add relevant tags here too.
- You can hashtag like crazy on **Instagram** and, really, the more the better. You can't add linking URLs here so be sure to just direct people to your website's blog or update the link in your bio.
- If there are lots of cool images in your blog post, then **Pinterest** is a good shout. People love repinning awesome photos, including well made header graphics with your blog post title or similar on them.

If you're really serious about getting your blog post some traction on social media then, as well as updating your social media platforms straight away, it's a good idea to schedule some posts for the future as well. This handy table shows how often you should share your post within 2 months after posting:

Table from Quicksprout

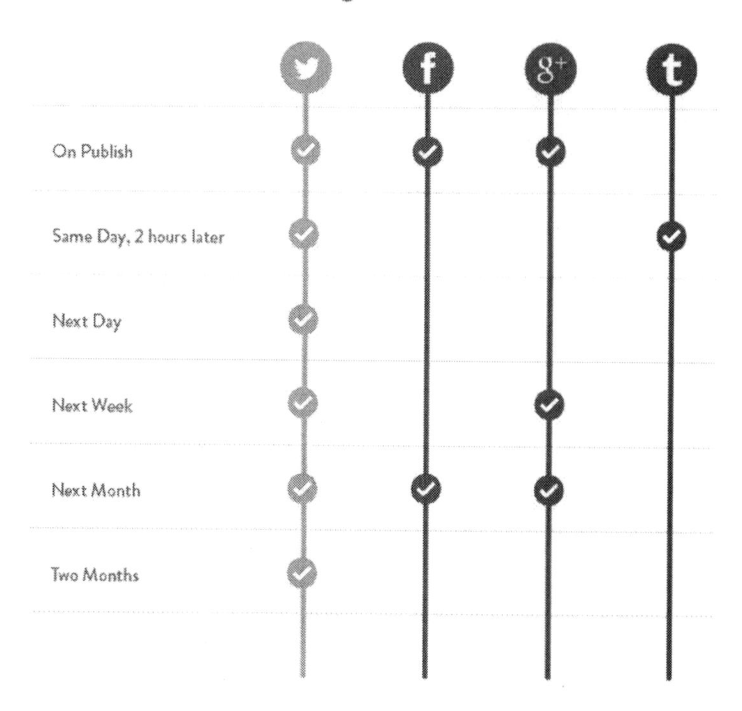

You can check out our new social media book, *Profitable Social Media Marketing: How To Grow Your Business Using Facebook, Twitter, Instagram, LinkedIn And More*, for more detail about optimum sharing of blog posts on social media platforms and how to utilise social media to promote your business and increase conversions.

Post to Aggregator Sites

Content aggregator sites are websites that collect a bunch of article links and highlight articles that they predict will be interesting to users. The point of content aggregator sites is to boost exposure and drive traffic back to the original website or blog where the articles were published. The most common aggregator websites include **Reddit, BlogLovin', StumbleUpon, Delicious** and **Digg**, although there may be more popular aggregator websites that are relevant to your specific niche or industry. For example, these are some of the leading aggregator site for business related niches:

- Inbound.org (Inbound marketing)
- Product Hunt (Product creation)
- Biz Sugar (Small business)
- Lobsters (Technology)

Something to beware of! Many aggregator websites are controlled by an editorial team and if you just post a bunch of links on the sites without actually contributing to the community, then your posts may just be flagged as spam. It's better to build up a reputation on these sites before trying to promote your business.

How Converting Readers to Customers Works

If you've followed all of the above steps and you now have a shiny new blog filled with visually stunning, well crafted, SEO optimised, valuable content, then it's time to start thinking about how you're actually going to convert readers into customers. When someone lands on your blog post, whether that's through search engines, social media, or well-placed backlinks from other blogs and websites, you've got a chance to convert these guys into paying customers. Here's the process to make that happen:

- Visitor is attracted to the website by a blog post
- Visitor reads the post and sees call-to-action for an offer of something free
- Visitor clicks call-to-action and is taken to a nice looking landing page, OR a call-to-action widget is embedded in the blog post
- Visitor fills out form with their email address, and receives the free offer

Neil Patel, the guy who runs content marketing blog QuickSprout and heatmap tool business Crazy Egg, is great at this stuff. Here's a screenshot from the end of one of Neil's most recent blog posts on QuickSprout:

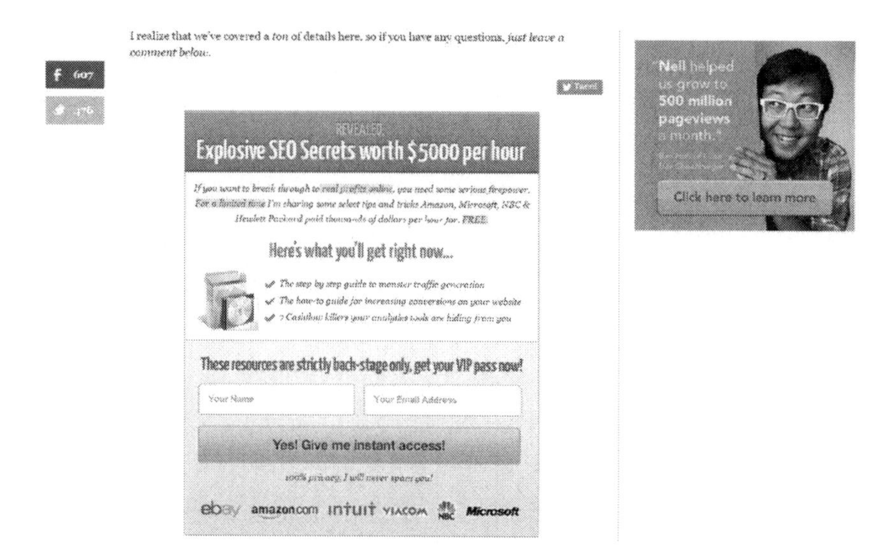

Before we even get to that awesome looking widget, take a look at the last line of the blog post: "I realize that we've covered a *ton* of details here, so if you have any questions, *just leave a comment below.*" That line is golden: it confirms to the reader that Neil is a nice guy, it encourages them to comment and engage with him as well, which gives him an extra chance to prove what an expert he is.

Then there's that detailed call-to-action box that is making it so, so simple for blog readers to whack in their details, sit back, and wait for the SEO secrets to come rolling into their inbox. He's highlighted the fact that it's for a limited time and it's FREE – what reader can resist free stuff, especially when they don't have long to get it!?

Take a look at the very beginning of a blog post on Crazy Egg:

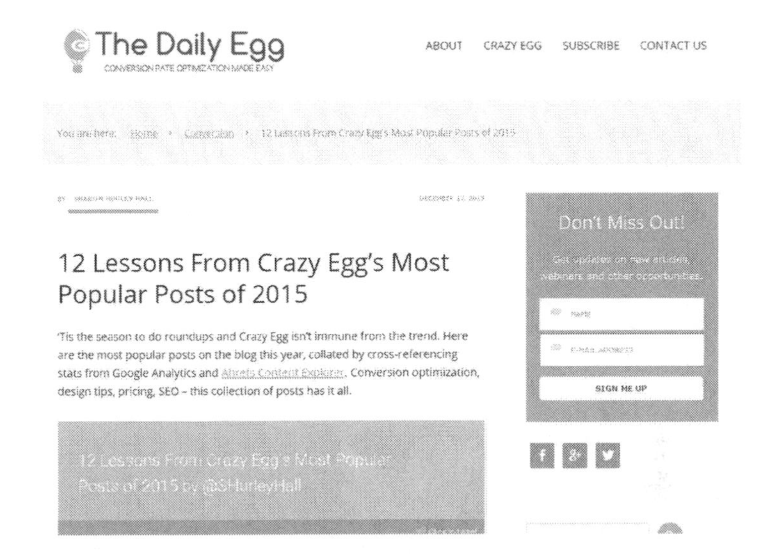

The call-to-action here features before we've even started reading the post! Yes, that bright green box sitting above the fold to the right of the screen is telling the reader not to miss out on signing up to Crazy Egg's newsletter. It's simple, it's easy, and it's big.

Here's an example from our very own Exposure Ninja blog. We've just finished writing our awesome social media marketing book (*you should check it out*) and we want to encourage blog readers to click over onto Amazon and grab a copy. Here's our call-to-action:

You can find more details on how to get the best out of your social media marketing via our new book Profitable Social Media Marketing: How To Grow Your Business

It's a big image with a big photo of the product we're talking about and a big red button. Not to mention that the word FREE is also featured here as we're offering a free marketing review to sweeten the deal.

Lush's blog goes one step even further with getting people to sign up to their newsletter. A big pop up takes over the whole screen when you land on their blog:

While it might seem like overkill, sign ups tend to be really high with this kind of tactic as well.

Really Want to Get Your Blog Post Ranking?

So you wrote a super awesome, SEO-friendly blog post on and you want to get it ranking higher on the search engines for your client! Great stuff. What do you do? You build links to it in articles. You can write articles about related topics that you're pitching to editors. When writing your articles, include links to your blog post within the content of those articles.

Say we just wrote a blog post for on "5 Secret Greek Islands You Must Visit This Summer" for our Greek tour company business. Now, we can pitch and write an article for The Greek Reporter on "How to Plan a Summer Holiday to Greece". In that article, we could mention visiting secret Greek islands or unmissable Greek islands for summer holidays and link back to our blog post within the article.

When that gets published – great. We're signalling to Google through our anchor text (the words in the link) and the attached link URL that the page is a great resource for that topic. And that will help boost rankings for that page.

Measuring Your Blog's ROI

While you're not going to see a return on your investment on day one of blogging, over time you should start to see a steady increase of traffic, a lower bounce rate, lots of click throughs, and some conversions coming through.

Is your blog resulting in increased traffic to your website?

This is the first question. Most businesses won't be trying to convert directly from a blog post but instead getting more people onto and browsing around the website. If you're getting lots of users landing on blog pages, then your honeypot is attracting the bees. You can check this on your **Google Analytics** dashboard.

Are you seeing increased engagement?

Are your readers commenting on and/or sharing blog posts on social media? You can make a quick calculation based on the time/cost of writing each blog post and divide that by the number of social media shares to work out an average cost per share. You can compare this reach to other social media posts and marketing channels.

Is your blog generating leads?

While blog posts are very rarely used to directly gain conversions, they can be a great source of leads. What do you want blog readers to do? Are you asking readers to subscribe to a newsletter, visit product pages, buy a product, email or call about your services, download an e-book etc? You can use Google Analytics to keep track of click through rates, email signup etc to see if you're getting the desired results.

Not seeing a decent ROI yet?

If after three months or so of blogging, you're not starting to see any movement then you need to take a closer look at what kind of content you're producing – is it valuable to your readers? Are you targeting the right readership? Are you actually reaching this audience? It's likely that there will be a flaw in either the substance (post content), the delivery (how good your blog looks), the reach (getting the post to your audience), or the offer (your website's lead generation).

Using Heatmaps

If you think that you're doing everything right but the people on your website just don't seem to be clicking around or converting, then you might want to run a heatmap. Heatmaps can be used to see what parts of the page people ignore and what they spend most of their time looking at. You can use a free trial of an online heatmap tool like **Crazy Egg** for this.

Your Digital PR Plan

The hardest part of digital PR is getting started. This book as a whole heap of information and advice that you've probably not considered in a whole lot of detail before and we totally get that it can be very overwhelming when you're starting out. What's important is to remember when it comes to digital PR is that you don't have to get it *perfect*; you just have to get it *going*. Once you start, you can work out what works and what doesn't making adjustments along the way.

If you've got to here and you're not quite sure how to crack on, flick back to the start of this book and follow the action points. These are step-by-step actions that will support you in forming and implementing a digital PR plan for your business. These actions points involve identifying your target audience, setting out your goals, deciding which strategies are most relevant to your business, creating a PR schedule, researching article topics and publications, and reaching out to editors and bloggers.

Don't forget that the very first action point is to claim your FREE marketing review at www.exposureninja.com/review.

Day-To-Day PR Management

It can be tempting to go totally gung-ho for digital PR and be shooting out emails left, right, and centre just whenever you have some spare time between other work tasks. But a slap-dash approach usually leads to mistakes and you might find yourself accidentally sending out copy and pasted emails that say "Hi Claire" to five different bloggers who aren't called Claire.

Instead, set aside a time slot twice a week or so to dedicate to PR work, and another to dedicate to writing blogs for your own website. You're better off getting "in the zone" and focusing properly on your business' PR tactics if you want them to have a positive impact – otherwise you're just throwing away your time.

Allocate time to checking and responding to PR related emails as well. The back-and-forth involved in emailing editors and bloggers can start eating up time faster than Pac-Man swallows Pac-dots. You can use an email took like **Streak** (an extension for Gmail) to organise your digital PR opportunities and leads into different folders and stages (called pipelines), so that they're easier to keep track of and pick up on again later.

DIY Digital PR vs Outsourcing

The decision of whether to run your digital PR campaign yourself or outsource it is an important one. Generally we recommend that if you *want* to do it yourself, that probably means you should at least give it a go.

Some people will read this book, like the sound of what is mentioned, but will be thinking that running a digital PR campaign is just too time consuming to take on themselves. Others will have the best intentions, but the reality is that once "real life" kicks in and they are in the day to day of their business, they just won't find the time and their digital PR campaign will die out slowly. For these business owners, outsourcing is the way to go. Freelance PR specialists, blogger outreach specialists, article writers and blog content writers can be hired on websites like **UpWork**, **Elance**, and **Fiverr**.

If you're worried about how to go about finding a good freelancer or concerned about the quality of work, the other outsourcing option is to find a reputable digital marketing company who have a digital PR department. These companies – like all us ninjas here at Exposure Ninja – specialise in handling multiple areas of your digital marketing, including digital PR, SEO, social media, paid advertising, and website development. Any good company will let you pick and choose the services you need and tailor a digital marketing package to suit your needs.

If you decide to outsource your digital marketing elsewhere (because you don't want a ninja campaign, for whatever crazy reason), then here are some tips for choosing a provider:

- Hire a native English speaker or a second language speaker with impeccable English. Don't fall into the trap of hiring the cheapest freelancer you can find. When a company hires the cheapest guy from India going on $2 per hour to write their articles, those articles are going to be completely worthless and so are any pitches that they send out – you may as well start a bonfire with that money and forget running a digital PR campaign altogether. Look for a good value freelancer – a fair price for you and them – and ask to see a portfolio of their previous work.

- Make sure that your freelancers or digital PR company make an effort to understand your business before they get started. There is nothing worse than a generic PR strategy that makes no attempt to demonstrate expertise or demonstrates your expertise in all the wrong areas. You're unlikely to find a freelancer right off the bat that knows the inside outs of your industry. Still, as long as they have the writing experience and put in the work, they can become experts in it – our own ninjas come from a range of writing backgrounds and have learned to write incredible content for just about every kind of small business out there. If you work in a very complicated or specialised industry, then you may need to give more input to initial topic ideas, pitches, and articles.

- Be clear about what is and isn't covered in your plan. Some freelancers work only as article writers, while others specialise only in the contacting and pitching of ideas to publications. You can find freelancers who do both, but make sure to double check with them. If your campaign is extending into social media and/or SEO work as well, it may be worth looking for an online marketing specialist who has skills in multiple areas. You could also consider outsourcing all your online marketing work to a digital marketing company who deal with multiple areas.

- Measure the numbers that are important to you (ROI rather than cost). All that matters to your business is the money that your digital PR campaign brings in compared to what it costs. It makes no sense to artificially restrict a PR budget if spending just a little more could bring in a multiple of the return. Of course you don't want to go crazy and break the bank, but pinching pennies in marketing generally shows a focus on the wrong thing – the cost – rather than the true goal – the return.

- Be wary of guarantees. Just like SEO, you'll find companies who are more than happy to guarantee results – be it the number of links, named publications/bloggers you can get into etc – and while it's one thing a company being confident about getting results, be wary that they're making guarantees about things which they can't control and assumptions that may be incorrect. A guarantee usually suggests a company who are doing anything just to make a sale or who will be doing some dodgy activities on your behalf that will come back to haunt you later on. Fake social media followers, black hat SEO techniques, link farms, fake traffic and so on are all pointless exercises that won't benefit your business.
- Have realistic expectations. Getting in big name publication or working with big name bloggers takes time and money. Don't expect to be on Forbes' front page after just one week of digital PR work. It takes time to reach out, establish your reputation, and build relationships with influencers in your industry. Discuss with your freelancer about any contacts who you already have on your books (where you pay to advertise, friends who run businesses in the local areas etc.) and see if they have experience writing for any of your target publications. When you outsource for a set amount of hours, think about what could realistically be achieved in that time and discuss timescales and budget with the outsourcer.
- Think carefully about long-term contracts. While it obviously takes time for the effects of any campaign to bear fruit, you will be able to see within a couple months how effective your outsourced digital PR company is. Ask to be kept in the loop regularly or for a round-up of work achieved each week or month (depending how many hours you've allocated to your PR work). You don't want to be paying for an ineffective or incompetent freelancer or company for longer than you have to. If the company is confident in the quality of their work, they won't see any need to bind you into a long-term contract.

Next Steps

Now it's up to you! Carve your own digital PR path and take your market by storm – remember that you can call on our digital PR ninjas anytime with questions about digital PR and content marketing for your business, whatever they are!

Not only that, but we're happy to offer you a **completely free of charge** website and marketing review – whether or not you already have a digital PR plan in place. This review will take a look at your existing positioning and make some suggestions about how you can use your website and digital PR to make you absolutely killer in your market.

To claim your free marketing review, head on over to www.exposureninja.com/review

Our team of online marketing ninjas are the sharpest in the business, and we love nothing more than getting a big fat juicy testimonial from a client who we've saved or a small business owner like you who is about to dominate the online world. If you enjoyed this book, I'd really appreciate a review on Amazon. It makes a big difference, and we enjoy reading them.

If you're not happy with the book in any way, let me know why and I'll personally refund you the cost of the book if you don't consider it a good investment. Just drop me an email and we'll get it sorted :-)

If you have any comments, suggestions, or feedback you can contact me personally by email tim@exposureninja.com

Digital PR & Content Marketing Tools

We've put together this handy glossary of tools we mentioned in the book that are useful for digital PR campaigns.

Backlink Watch *(backlinkwatch.com)*
Research backlinks on any website and analyse competitor backlink profiles. Behind the spammy-looking exterior is a useful piece of kit!

Bloglovin' *(bloglovin.com)*
News feed management tool for following blogs and researching influential bloggers.

Buffer *(buffer.com)*
Social media management tool that can be used to schedule updates in advance.

Buzzstream *(buzzstream.com)*
Digital outreach management tool.

Buzzsumo *(buzzsumo.com)*
Find most shared content and discover influencers. The free version gives you a very limited experience, but may be suitable for businesses that are just getting started with content creation.

Canva ***(canva.com)***
Image editing tool which can be used to design graphics and marketing materials and to overlay text on images.

Crazy Egg ***(crazyegg.com)***
Heatmap software to see where website users look and click most when on a webpage.

Delicious ***(delicious.com)***
Social bookmarking website to save and add interesting links.

Digg ***(digg.com)***
Popular and viral content discovery engine.

Evernote ***(evernote.com)***
App designed for note taking and organising.

Feedly ***(feedly.com)***
Compiles customisable news feeds from online sources including blogs.

Fiverr ***(uk.fiverr.com)***
Find creative and professional services for website graphics, logos, marketing materials, videos, animations, and other creative services.

Flickr ***(flickr.com)***
Stock photo website. Advanced search function allows users to find images that are under the Creative Commons license and can be used for free with attribution to the photographer.

Followerwonk ***(moz.com/followerwonk)***
Twitter analytics tool which allows users to search and compare Twitter profiles.

Gleam ***(gleam.io)***
App to run giveaways and competitions on websites and blogs.

Google Alerts ***(google.co.uk/alerts)***
Get notifications for new content published on a certain topic or keyword.

Google Analytics *(google.co.uk/analytics)*
Web analytics services that track and report on website traffic.

Google Insights *(google.co.uk/insights)*
Useful tool for tracking and comparing trends.

Google News *(news.google.co.uk)*
Search for most recent news stories from news based websites.

Google Trends *(google.co.uk/trends)*
See how often a set of keywords are Googled, enabling you to see what is trending and how that trend has changed over time. It also predicts how the trend may change in the future, and you can compare different keyword sets to one another. This resource is excellent and free.

GroupHigh *(grouphigh.com)*
Blogger outreach management software.

Hootsuite *(hootsuite.com)*
Social media management tool that can be used to scheduled updates in advance.

InkyBee *(inkybee.com)*
Blogger outreach and digital outreach management software.

Moz Open Site Explorer *(moz.com/researchtools/ose)*
Research backlinks on any website, analyse competitor backlink profiles, and measure a website's domain authority.

Piktochart *(piktochart.com)*
Create infographics, reports, and presentations online. Both free and paid versions.

Pixabay *(pixabay.com)*
Stock photo website.

Pixlr *(pixlr.com)*
Image editing tool which can be used to edit photos and design graphics.

Rafflecopter ***(rafflecopter.com)***
App to run giveaways and competitions on websites and blogs.

Reddit ***(reddit.com)***
Social networking and news website where blog content can be shared.

Response Source ***(responsesource.com)***
A paid-for enquiry service for journalists and PR people. Used by all the major national newspapers in the UK. Worth the money only for companies that are seriously dedicated to PR.

SEM Rush ***(semrush.com)***
Check organic keywords for any website.

Shutterstock ***(shutterstock.com)***
Stock photo website.

Stock Snap ***(stocksnap.io)***
Stock photo website.

Streak ***(streak.com)***
An extension for Gmail which lets you organise emails and workflow with folders, boxes, and pipelines.

StumbleUpon ***(stumbleupon.com)***
Social network and personalised blog discovery engine.

Trello Boards ***(trello.com)***
Save links you like and organise your projects into boards.

Quantcast ***(quantcast.com)***
Audience measurement and insights software for websites and blogs.

Unsplash ***(unsplash.com)***
Stock photo website.

UpWork ***(upwork.com)***
Hire freelancers for web-based projects, including blog writers, web designers, graphic designers, outreach specialists, content marketers etc.

Yoast ***(yoast.com)***
SEO plugin for Wordpress. Helps users to optimise SEO on webpages and blog posts.

17829167R00119

Printed in Great Britain
by Amazon